BOOT CAMP
FOR THE ACT®

BETTER SCORES IN ONE DAY

4th Edition

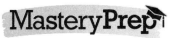

MasteryPrep
7117 Florida Blvd.
Baton Rouge, LA 70806

10 9 8 7 6 5 4 3 2 1

ISBN-13: 978-1-948846-92-9

Table of Contents

In 2003, I made perfect scores on the ACT and the SAT. Since that time, I've helped students like you boost their ACT scores. I've helped students scoring as low as a 13 and as high as a 33 get the scores that they needed.

My experience in helping students led me to develop the Mastery for the ACT program. Mastery for the ACT is the fastest-growing ACT prep program in the nation, and it's used in schools throughout the U.S. to help students improve their scores.

Mastery for the ACT is a comprehensive program. It answers a lot of questions. One question it didn't answer, however, was this: "I'm taking the ACT in two days. What do I need to learn?"

Our only answer before this Boot Camp for the ACT was for you to step into a time machine, go back a couple months, and start working through Mastery for the ACT.

Now, I can tell you without reservation—if you are lacking in the time machine department—to do the Boot Camp for the ACT. This program is designed to give you the ultimate one-day cram.

I've written the Boot Camp for the ACT to help you. If I were tutoring you personally, we would go over the information in this workshop right before your test date.

With this Boot Camp, you can learn the skills that you need to boost your scores on the ACT.

My path to perfect scores on the ACT and the SAT was not a smooth one. My education, you could say, happened in a rapid series of fits and starts. Occasionally, I did a good job of pacing myself with my school work, but for every one time that happened, there were 20 times where I was cramming the night before (or even the day of) the test.

I do best under pressure. I've come to realize that this is also the case for most of the students I work with. You can call it simply "waiting until the last minute," but I think there is a human instinct that kicks in, a survival mechanism of sorts, that clears your head and helps you to get done what needs to be done.

My Mastery for the ACT program is designed to gradually build your skills to a level of mastery of the ACT. If you have months to prepare, get started on Mastery for the ACT right after this Boot Camp.

This workshop is for the "final hours." It's here because the truth is that it's a rare student who is able to fit in gradual, steady ACT prep into his or her hectic schedule. Sometimes the best prep comes just before the test begins. It isn't a replacement for long-term ACT prep (which you'll need to make large gains on your scores), but the Boot Camp for the ACT will guide you through the essentials on pacing, test-taking strategies, and the question types missed most on the ACT.

I've taken research based on what thousands of my students have missed on actual ACT tests and distilled that information down into this workshop. It's designed to give you everything you need—and nothing that you don't—quickly enough that you can cover it all in a single day.

— Craig Gehring, CEO and Founder of MasteryPrep

Boot Camp for the ACT®
Schedule

Fill in the times following your instructor's directions. This is the agenda we will follow throughout the day. We'll have a break between each section. Next to each section name in the schedule, you'll find the corresponding page number where it begins in this workbook.

TIME	SECTION	PAGE
_____	ACT Overview	7
_____	English	13
_____	Math	67
_____	Break	
_____	Reading	123
_____	Science	155
_____	Writing	187
_____	Boot Camp Wrap-Up	193

ACT
Overview

» A MILLION REASONS FOR HIGHER ACT SCORES

- On average, college graduates earn a million dollars more than high school graduates over the course of their lifetimes.

- Your ACT score helps you to gain college entrance and scholarships.

- It is at least as important to admission boards as your grade point average and class rank. With all of the work that you put into your high school courses, you owe it to yourself to make a serious effort to boost your ACT scores.

- The higher your score, the more likely it is that you'll get a degree.

- You can't rely on your teachers to do this for you. It's your job to build your future.

Why do you want higher ACT scores?

What ACT score do you want? _____

Do you know how many extra points you need? If so, write that in this blank. _____

NOTES

_____

_____

_____

_____

_____

_____

_____

_____

_____

» ORIENTATION

The ACT is a marathon of a test. Between the English, Math, Reading, Science, and optional Writing tests, you'll spend over 3 hours answering more than 200 questions designed to determine how ready you are for college.

Sequence	Subject	Questions	Passages	Time
1	English	75	5	45 minutes
2	Math	60	-	60 minutes
Break	-	-	-	10-15 minutes
3	Reading	40	4	35 minutes
4	Science	40	6 or 7	35 minutes
5	Writing	1	-	40 minutes

English tests your ability to edit writing.

Math measures your ability to solve complicated word problems.

Reading checks how well you interpret and comprehend reading passages.

Science doesn't determine whether you know science facts, but rather how well you read scientific information and infographics.

Writing demonstrates how well you can write a sophisticated argument on the spot.

» HOW THE ACT IS SCORED

- The ACT is scored in an odd way.

- You need to understand exactly how it's scored so that you can make and achieve realistic goals for improvement.

- **Don't prep only for your weakest subjects. A balanced approach to ACT prep is necessary.**

SAMPLE CONVERSION TABLE

Scale Score	Raw Scores			
	Test 1 English	Test 2 Mathematics	Test 3 Reading	Test 4 Science
36	75	60	40	40
35	74	59	39	39
34	73	58	39	39
33	72	58	38	38
32	71	57	37	38
31	71	55	37	38
30	69	53	36	37
29	68	52	35	36
28	67	50	34	36
27	65	47	33	34
26	63	45	32	33
25	61	42	31	31
24	59	40	30	30
23	57	37	29	28
22	54	36	27	27
21	52	34	26	25
20	49	32	24	23
19	46	30	22	21
18	43	28	21	19
17	41	25	19	17
16	38	20	18	15
15	35	17	16	14
14	33	14	14	13
13	31	12	13	12
12	29	9	12	11
11	26	7	10	10
10	24	6	8	8
9	21	5	7	7
8	18	4	6	6
7	15	3	5	5
6	12	3	4	4
5	9	2	4	3
4	7	1	3	2
3	5	1	2	1
2	3	1	1	1
1	0	0	0	0

How many questions do you need to answer correctly in order to score a 20 in the English test? _____

Circle the number of questions you need to answer correctly on this chart in each test to get the ACT composite score that you want.

SECTION TWO
English

» AN INTRODUCTION TO THE ACT ENGLISH TEST

- The ACT English test is made up of five passages and 75 questions that challenge your editing ability.

- Some questions check your knowledge of **grammar** while others test your **composition skills**.

- The ACT English test is one of the most demanding tests in terms of time.

Look at page 18. What is the question number of a composition question? _____

What is the question number of a grammar question? _____

NOTES

_____

_____

_____

_____

_____

_____

_____

_____

_____

_____

_____

_____

_____

_____

» HOW DO I MANAGE MY TIME?

- With only 45 minutes to answer 75 questions, you must answer a question every 30 seconds.

- An easier way to keep track of it is this: **Give yourself 8 minutes per passage.**

- If you maintain this pace, you'll get through the entire test with 5 minutes to spare.

- Most students miss the last questions because they run out of time. Get through each passage in 8 minutes, and you'll never run out of time on the ACT English test.

- Part of managing your time is knowing when to skip a question. **If you don't know the answer, mark and move.** Chances are that the next question is easier.

- You'll get way more questions right if you give yourself the chance to complete the entire test.

- Another part of getting through the English test with sufficient time is to practice thinking and working at the correct pace. The only way to accomplish this is to **move at the correct pace while you are practicing.**

In this Boot Camp we'll do a number of practice tests designed to help you understand ACT content and move at the correct pace. When you're working through the tests, pretend that you are actually in an ACT test environment.

Check your understanding:

How many minutes should you allow for each passage?_____

When you do the first mini-test, try to identify questions that you need to skip so that you can better manage your time and get to the end of the passage before time runs out.

» THE ART OF GUESSING

- There is no penalty whatsoever for guessing on the ACT.

- Never *ever* leave an answer blank.

- **Mark and move.**

- Again, *never* leave an answer blank. If you read the question and decide to skip it, fill in your best guess before moving to the next question.

- **Eliminate the answers that are most unlikely** and go with your gut.

- By guessing as you go, you'll have most of the answers completed when you reach the test's end.

- Your guesses will be much better right after you read the question than if you wait until the end of the test and blindly guess.

Mark the question in your test booklet so you can come back to it, make your best guess, and **then** move on.

Be sure to apply this technique with the mini-tests in the Boot Camp. Only with practice will this feel natural. Use this technique to guess twice as well without any more effort.

NOTES

_____

_____

_____

_____

_____

_____

_____

_____

_____

_____

_____

» INTRODUCING BOOT CAMP FOR THE ACT MINI-TESTS

- You will be taking a small segment of an ACT test.

- It's important to **imagine that you are in an actual ACT environment**.

- The time limit matches the pace that you should try to beat during the actual ACT.

- **Practice all of the skills that you've learned as you do these mini-tests.**

- In this mini-test, you're provided 8 minutes to answer 15 questions related to one English passage.

- Unless your instructor has provided you with an answer sheet, circle your answers directly in this book.

- Your instructor will call out times and recommendations of what question you should be on or have already completed. It's OK if you get a little ahead or behind the numbered question the instructor is calling out. Try to get all the way through under the time limit.

- The real test does not allow the use of cell phones, watches, or scratch paper, so you shouldn't use them on the mini-tests either.

ENGLISH TEST
45 Minutes — 75 Questions

DIRECTIONS: In the passages to follow, selected words or phrases will be underlined. The selection will have a corresponding number in the right-hand column. You will be given alternatives and are expected to choose one as the best replacement for the original selection.

Often, the correct answer will be one that best articulates the idea, maintains the tone and style of the passage, or is considered most appropriate for standard written English. If you believe the original to be correct, choose "NO CHANGE."

Other times, you will be questioned on the passage as a whole, which is indicated not by an underlined portion, but by one or more numbers in a box.

Choose the answer you believe to be correct, then color its corresponding bubble on your answer sheet. Before beginning, read the passage at least once, as some questions refer to several parts before or after the selected phrase. Repeat this for each question to ensure you have read enough ahead to choose the right alternative.

PASSAGE I

Farther

The shimmering beach extends endlessly into the horizon. Emerald waves creep along the white sands like eels
curving, and bending along the seashore.
1

Years ago, the city dictated that the dunes must be
protected—not taken for granted—so
2

they could enjoy the natural beauty of the area for years to
3
come.

I walk the same stretch of beach every morning, where the warmth of the sun gently awakens me. I have come to love this routine and cherish it deeply. Today, I'm ready to
4
walk farther than I ever have

1. A. NO CHANGE
    B. eels, curving and bending
    C. eels curving and bending,
    D. eels, curving, and bending,

2. **F.** NO CHANGE
    G. protected; not taken for granted
    H. protected not taken for granted
    J. protected, not taken for granted;

3. A. NO CHANGE
    B. knowing they
    C. that they
    D. people

4. Which of the following alternatives to the underlined portion would NOT be acceptable?
    F. routine, cherishing
    G. routine and always cherish
    H. routine, always cherishing
    J. routined cherish

GO ON TO THE NEXT PAGE.

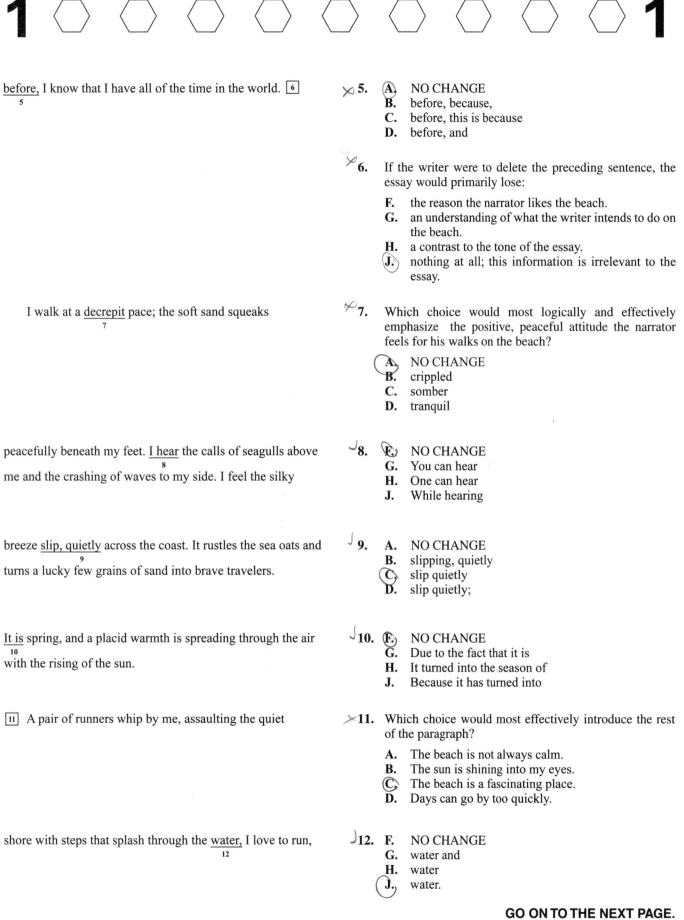

before, I know that I have all of the time in the world. [6]
5

I walk at a decrepit pace; the soft sand squeaks
7

peacefully beneath my feet. I hear the calls of seagulls above
8
me and the crashing of waves to my side. I feel the silky

breeze slip, quietly across the coast. It rustles the sea oats and
9
turns a lucky few grains of sand into brave travelers.

It is spring, and a placid warmth is spreading through the air
10
with the rising of the sun.

[11] A pair of runners whip by me, assaulting the quiet

shore with steps that splash through the water, I love to run,
12

5. **A.** NO CHANGE
B. before, because,
C. before, this is because
D. before, and

6. If the writer were to delete the preceding sentence, the essay would primarily lose:
F. the reason the narrator likes the beach.
G. an understanding of what the writer intends to do on the beach.
H. a contrast to the tone of the essay.
J. nothing at all; this information is irrelevant to the essay.

7. Which choice would most logically and effectively emphasize the positive, peaceful attitude the narrator feels for his walks on the beach?
A. NO CHANGE
B. crippled
C. somber
D. tranquil

8. **F.** NO CHANGE
G. You can hear
H. One can hear
J. While hearing

9. **A.** NO CHANGE
B. slipping, quietly
C. slip quietly
D. slip quietly;

10. **F.** NO CHANGE
G. Due to the fact that it is
H. It turned into the season of
J. Because it has turned into

11. Which choice would most effectively introduce the rest of the paragraph?
A. The beach is not always calm.
B. The sun is shining into my eyes.
C. The beach is a fascinating place.
D. Days can go by too quickly.

12. **F.** NO CHANGE
G. water and
H. water
J. water.

GO ON TO THE NEXT PAGE.

19

but today it is time to appreciate the serenity of this world. I want to watch quarter-sized crabs skitter across the sands and the dorsal fins of dolphins slice through the water in the distance. Today, I notice the new shapes that the beach has taken, the new ways in which it has chosen to twist and curve. I see new treasures of the sea, the shells and keepsakes and driftwood. Spending hours walking, I reach a place that I have never seen.

But at some point, I have to turn back to repeat the steps already taken, though completely in reverse. I see everything again with only the slightest variation. I reach my beach access and traverse its worn wooden steps back to reality. Here, lavish buildings, spotless streets, and manicured lawns wait for me in silence. I put my sandals back on and begin my paved journey back home. But as my sandals pitter-patter along the pavement, there is already the anticipation of tomorrow's walk. In my mind, there are memories of the glimmering waters, the smooth sands, and the brilliant sunlight. Tomorrow, I will walk farther than I ever have before.

13. **A.** NO CHANGE
    B. walking I reach
    C. walking, and I reach
    D. walking I reach:

14. **F.** NO CHANGE
    G. lawn's
    H. lawns'
    J. lawns's

> Question 15 asks about the preceding passage as a whole.

15. Suppose the writer's goal had been to write an essay illustrating the peaceful atmosphere of the beach. Would this essay accomplish that goal?

    A. Yes, because it focuses on various fish species that can be seen from the beach.
    B. Yes, because it focuses on the narrator's joy in taking long, quiet walks on the beach.
    C. No, because it says that the real world is more interesting than the beach.
    D. No, because it focuses more on the difference between running and walking.

END OF TEST
STOP! DO NOT GO ON TO THE NEXT PAGE
UNTIL TOLD TO DO SO.

» HEAD DOWN! USE EVERY MINUTE

- When you get through the test under the time limit, always use your remaining time to review your answers.

- Plug in answer choices and eliminate them to make sure you haven't made a mistake.

- **Keep your head down on the ACT and use every minute available, double—and triple—checking if you have time.**

- Practice doing this with all of the rest of the practice tests. (And continue to use the *guessing as you go* technique as well!)

Check your understanding: Why is it a good idea to use every minute on the ACT?

NOTES

_____

_____

_____

_____

_____

_____

_____

_____

_____

_____

_____

_____

_____

_____

_____

» SEMICOLONS: WHEN NOT TO USE THEM

Semicolons can be used as a sort of "Super Comma!" You can use them when an ordinary comma just won't do (for clarity's sake) or when you need a comma that will stand out from the other commas in the sentence.

> **EXAMPLE:** This summer, I visited Paris, France; Rome, Italy; and London, England.

The ACT almost never uses semicolons as super commas.

As many as six or seven questions on the ACT may have answer choices that include semicolons, *but only one or two uses are actually correct.*

- **A semicolon can be used instead of a period to join two independent clauses.**

This shows a tighter relationship between the clauses than if they were made into separate sentences.

That being said, it is grammatically correct to use a semicolon in this way only if you could also replace it with a period and have both clauses stand alone as complete sentences.

> **CORRECT:** I walked out of the store; it cost too much.
>
> **INCORRECT:** I walked out of the store; costing too much.

I walked out of the store and *it cost too much* can both stand alone as sentences. They're independent clauses.

Costing too much can't stand alone, so it's incorrect to use the semicolon here.

In other words, **if you can't replace the semicolon with a period, it's being used incorrectly on the ACT.** Let's look at question 2 as an example of this:

> **2.** Years ago, the city dictated that the dunes must be <u>protected—not taken for granted—</u>so they could enjoy the natural beauty of the area for years to come.
>
> F. NO CHANGE
>
> G. protected; not taken for granted
>
> H. protected not taken for granted
>
> J. protected, not taken for granted;

In this question, the semicolon could not be replaced with a period and leave two complete sentences, so choice G is incorrect. Choice J is incorrect because you should never use a semicolon before a coordinating conjunction unless you have internal commas within the independent clauses.

Note: It's also **incorrect to use a coordinating conjunction after a semicolon** in this way. Use this guide to weed out the incorrect semicolon usage strewn throughout the ACT.

> **CORRECT:** Joe gave his brother a big hug; he was overjoyed to see him.
>
> **INCORRECT:** Joe gave his brother a big hug; because he was overjoyed to see him.

» WHY YOUR WORDS' FEELINGS MATTER

Take a look at this question from the mini-test:

7. I walk at a <u>decrepit</u> pace; the soft sand squeaks peacefully beneath my feet.

Which choice would most logically and effectively emphasize the positive, peaceful attitude the narrator feels toward his walks on the beach?

A. NO CHANGE

B. crippled

C. somber

D. tranquil

Sometimes the author's **word choice** can make all the difference in what is communicated to the reader.

I could describe the same event using two different words and create a dramatically different effect.

"The car moved" and **"the car roared around the corner"** could be describing the same thing, but the second phrase evokes an image of a **powerful vehicle moving quickly** and creates a certain **emotion** or **feeling** in the reader.

In the example problem above, *somber*, *decrepit*, and *crippled* do not evoke positive, peaceful attitudes in the reader. Therefore, *tranquil* is your best bet.

- **Make word choices that create the effect that the author intends.**

» WHY ARE ALL OF THE ANSWERS RIGHT?

- **When more than one answer appears correct, it's time to re-evaluate what you're looking for.**

- If more than one answer is grammatically correct, then *look for what is the best choice in terms of composition*.

- If you're unsure between two grammatical choices, *go with the one that you feel more certain about*.

Find a question in the first mini-test on pages 18–20 where all of the answers are grammatically correct. _____

NOTES

_____

_____

_____

_____

_____

_____

_____

_____

_____

_____

_____

_____

_____

_____

_____

_____

This page intentionally left blank.

PASSAGE II

After the Golden Spike

[A] On <u>May 10th, 1869; a group</u> of government and
railroad officials gathered to view the Driving of the Last
Spike. Estimates of the number of attendees ranged from
as few as 500 to as many as 3,000. They were gathered to
witness an accomplishment that would go on to change the
face of the <u>nation; the</u>

<u>ceremony driving</u> of the final spike into the first
Transcontinental Railroad.

After a decade of exploration and planning, construction
began on the 1,907-mile railroad from San Francisco,
California, to Council Bluffs, Iowa, along the Missouri River. [19]
The majority of the railroad was constructed by Civil War
veterans and recent immigrants. [B] Large work gangs of
thousands of men were employed for the

<u>construction: as</u> laborers, blacksmiths, engineers, masons,
and cooks. Men of many other specialties were

<u>required for efficient construction.</u> Telegraph lines were
even built along the railway to allow for quick and constant
communication.

In the end, the <u>six year</u> construction of the railroad
took less than a decade, beginning in 1863 and finishing in
1869. This historical event was celebrated as one of the most

16. F. NO CHANGE
    G. May 10, 1869, a group,
    H. May 10, 1869; a group,
    J. May 10, 1869, a group

17. A. NO CHANGE
    B. nation the,
    C. nation: the
    D. nation the

18. F. NO CHANGE
    G. ceremonial driving
    H. ceremony, driving
    J. ceremoniously driving

19. The writer is concerned about the level of detail in the
    preceding sentence and is considering deleting the phrase
    "After a decade of exploration and planning." If the
    writer were to make this deletion, the paragraph would
    primarily lose information that:

    A. explains the cost of the construction of the railroad.
    B. exhibits the difficulty involved in the construction
       process.
    C. exhibits the amount of preparation that was required
       before beginning work on the railroad.
    D. explains the results of constructing the railroad.

20. F. NO CHANGE
    G. construction, as
    H. construction as
    J. construction as:

21. A. NO CHANGE
    B. pretty useful.
    C. employed in this way.
    D. able to do work on the railroad.

22. F. NO CHANGE
    G. six years
    H. six-year-long
    J. DELETE the underlined portion.

GO ON TO THE NEXT PAGE.

incredible achievements of man; to commemorate them,
23
"The Golden Spike" was fashioned.

In what is considered to be the first mass media event in history, a crowd of laborers and officials gathered to watch the final spike be driven into the railroad. [C] The lively crowd, at Promontory Summit watched as the Last Spike,
24
fashioned from 17.6 karat copper-alloyed gold, was dropped into a pre-drilled hole and gently tapped into place with
25
a silver hammer. A single word, "Done," was transmitted
25
across the telegraph lines, alerting the nation that the railroad had been completed.

[D] Despite the media attention given to the Golden Spike, the Transcontinental Railroad did not run completely from coast to coast until August of 1870, when the final connection was made. The first Transcontinental Railroad was open to the masses, many of them were excited about the
26
opportunity to travel from New York to San Francisco

on a single train. Before long, books written in New York
27
City could be found on shelves in San Francisco. Shipments

23. **A.** NO CHANGE
B. those,
C. it,
D. him,

24. **F.** NO CHANGE
G. crowd—at Promontory Summit
H. crowd, at Promontory Summit,
J. crowd at Promontory Summit

25. **A.** NO CHANGE
B. with a hammer that had been created out of silver.
C. with a silver hammer that would create an interesting image for those at the ceremony.
D. DELETE the underlined portion and end the sentence with a period.

26. **F.** NO CHANGE
G. of whom
H. of who
J. DELETE the underlined portion

27. **A.** NO CHANGE
B. For instance,
C. In example,
D. That is,

GO ON TO THE NEXT PAGE.

of Japanese tea typically traded on the West Coast could now be traded on the East Coast. With one great achievement, American trade and intellectual discourse had changed completely. 28

28. The writer wishes to add one more sentence about the effect of the first Transcontinental Railroad on the United States' intellectual discourse. Given that all the following statements are true, which one, if added here, would most clearly and effectively accomplish the writer's goal?

F. By bringing the western states firmly and profitably into the Union, the Transcontinental Railroad greatly improved the economic situation in the United States.

G. The completion of the railroad allowed for the spreading of ideas throughout the United States at a much quicker pace.

H. The railroad was built by three private companies.

J. The first Transcontinental Railroad was commonly referred to as the Overland Route.

29. Upon reviewing the essay and finding that some information has been left out, the writer composes the following sentence incorporating that information:

Leland Stanford, American tycoon and founder of Stanford University, was chosen to be the man who would drive this final spike.

If the writer were to add this sentence to the essay, it would most logically be placed at point:

A. A
B. B
C. C
D. D

END OF TEST
STOP! DO NOT GO ON TO THE NEXT PAGE
UNTIL TOLD TO DO SO.

This page intentionally left blank.

» THE DIFFERENCE BETWEEN THE RIGHT ANSWER & THE BEST ANSWER

Stop looking for the "right" answer choice, and **start looking for the "best" answer choice.**

The best answer choice has nothing grammatically incorrect in it, is consistent with the passage, and communicates what the author means.

It's the most concise choice: the one that provides the most meaning in the fewest words.

All of the answers may be "correct," but **there will always be one answer choice that is "most correct."**

If you find yourself debating between two or three different possibilities that all look correct to you, try to narrow it down with these criteria:

The best answer choice:

- has nothing wrong with the **grammar**.

- is **consistent**.

- clearly **communicates**.

- is **concise**.

NOTES

_____

_____

_____

_____

_____

_____

_____

_____

_____

_____

_____

» COLONS: DON'T LET THEM FOOL YOU

Take a look at the following question from the mini-test:

17. They were gathered to witness an accomplishment that would go on to change the face of the <u>nation; the</u> ceremony driving of the final spike into the first Transcontinental Railroad.

    A. NO CHANGE

    B. nation the,

    C. nation: the

    D. nation the

- **A colon is like a gate or friendly sign, inviting the reader to go on.**

It says, "Beyond here lies the information you seek."

Typically, what comes after a colon is an example, further information, or a list.

- **For the purposes of the ACT, a colon can't be used to separate a subject from its verb, and it shouldn't interrupt a predicate.**

    INCORRECT: I went: to the store and bought eggs, milk, and honey.

    INCORRECT: I went to the store and bought: eggs, milk, and honey.

    CORRECT: I bought the following items from the store: eggs, milk, and honey.

- **The part of a sentence that comes before a colon must be able to stand on its own as a complete sentence.**

Often, what comes after a colon is a list.

In question 17, using a colon is appropriate because what comes before the colon stands on its own as a complete sentence, and what comes after provides further information on exactly what the accomplishment is that the author is talking about.

Using a semicolon, choice A, is incorrect because the second part of the sentence is not an independent clause. The comma in choice B is misplaced because it incorrectly interrupts the phrase [*ceremonial driving*] from its article, *the*. Using no punctuation, choice D, creates a run-on sentence.

» 20% OF YOUR ENGLISH SCORE HINGES ON THIS LITTLE MARK

24. The lively <u>crowd, at Promontory Summit</u> watched as the Last Spike, fashioned from 17.6 karat copper-alloyed gold, was dropped into a pre-drilled hole and gently tapped into place with a silver hammer.

F. NO CHANGE

G. crowd—at Promontory Summit

H. crowd, at Promontory Summit,

J. crowd at Promontory Summit

This question is a great illustration of the point:

- **Comma usage is the key to a higher ACT score.**

It's important that you're familiar with all of the grammar rules concerning commas. Below are a few guiding principles for dealing with commas on the ACT. Our Comma Boot Camp starts on the next page and includes seven essential comma rules.

- **On the ACT, more often than not you'll need to remove unnecessary commas rather than add essential commas.**

- **When in doubt, commas out.**

- **Commas are used to separate ideas.**

- **Commas cause pauses.**

- **No solo comma.**

- **Use commas to set off non-essential phrases from the part of the sentence they modify, but don't use commas for essential phrases.**

As many as 15 of the questions on the ACT English test concern commas in some fashion.

In question 24, the best answer is choice J. No comma or other punctuation mark is necessary between the noun *crowd* and the prepositional phrase that modifies it, *at Promontory Summit*. Choices F, G, and H are all incorrect for basically the same reason: they interrupt the connection between the noun and the prepositional phrase that modifies it.

1. Independent Clauses

INCORRECT: Lakesha bought 13 apples and Derrick purchased seven oranges.

CORRECT: Lakesha bought 13 apples, and Derrick purchased seven oranges.

Why? Use commas to separate independent clauses joined by the following conjunctions:

and   *but*   *for*   *or*   *nor*   *so*   *yet*

INCORRECT: I played basketball all weekend but I had to go back to work on Monday.

CORRECT: I played basketball all weekend, but I had to go back to work on Monday.

---

2. Introductory Words, Phrases, and Clauses

INCORRECT: After he lost the game he wasn't very talkative.

CORRECT: After he lost the game, he wasn't very talkative.

Why? Use commas after introductory clauses, phrases, and words.

In this case, *after he lost the game* is an introductory clause.

INCORRECT: Erica's voice was hoarse. However she still gave the song her best shot.

CORRECT: Erica's voice was hoarse. However, she still gave the song her best shot.

The main exception to this rule is if the introductory phrase is a prepositional phrase with four or fewer words.

Just because it has four or fewer words does not mean that you can omit the comma. It has to be a *prepositional phrase.*

One other note: be careful that you don't mistake an introductory phrase for a subject. You can never separate a subject from its verb with a single comma.

> **INCORRECT**: Trying to plan your life without any real experience, can lead you down the wrong path.
>
> **CORRECT**: Trying to plan your life without any real experience can lead you down the wrong path.

It sounds to the ear like the first portion of the sentence is a lead-in, but *trying to plan your life* functions as a subject that is modified by the prepositional phrase *without any real experience.*

---

3. Setting Off Asides

> **INCORRECT**: They visited the town of Gumpton, which for a long time had gone without any visitors in order to pay their respects to their dear aunt.
>
> **CORRECT**: They visited the town of Gumpton, which for a long time had gone without any visitors, in order to pay their respects to their dear aunt.

Why? Use two commas in the middle of a sentence in order to set off a phrase that is not essential to the meaning of the sentence.

The first comma goes where you start the aside, and the second comma goes at the end.

It helps to imagine that the narrator of the story stops what he's talking about for a second, cups his hand so that the characters don't hear, and tells you some interesting background information about one of them.

The action of the sentence pauses while we read some extra info. If you don't wrap it in two commas, you won't let your reader know where the pause in the action begins and ends.

INCORRECT: I drove my car a beat-up old Mustang to the end of the road.

CORRECT: I drove my car, a beat-up old Mustang, to the end of the road.

Don't set off phrases that are essential to the meaning of the sentence. With essential phrases, the action of the sentence doesn't pause. You're still telling the reader exactly what he needs to know, so don't confuse him by acting as if the information is just an aside.

INCORRECT: People, who don't work, don't have the benefit of a regular paycheck.

CORRECT: People who don't work don't have the benefit of a regular paycheck.

In this sentence, *who don't work* lets you know what people you're talking about. This phrase is essential to the meaning of the sentence, so don't treat it like an aside. No commas are necessary in this case.

---

4. Separating Equal Adjectives

INCORRECT: Jody's pit bull was a friendly warm animal, except toward post office employees.

CORRECT: Jody's pit bull was a friendly, warm animal, except toward post office employees.

The adjectives *friendly* and *warm* both modify *animal*. They're both equally important. One doesn't contribute to the meaning of the other. For that reason, you have to separate them with a comma in order to avoid confusion for the reader.

These are called coordinate adjectives.

When in doubt, ask yourself these two questions: Can I write these adjectives in reverse order? Can I interject the word "and" between the two adjectives? If the answer is "yes" to both of these questions, then you need to use a comma to separate them.

Don't use a comma to separate adjectives that depend on one another.

INCORRECT: Hannah ditched her red, wool hat in favor of a more subtle purple one.

CORRECT: Hannah ditched her red wool hat in favor of a more subtle purple one.

In this case, the adjectives are not equal. You can't reverse the order to say "wool red hat." Well, you can, but it doesn't make much sense!

---

5. Don't Separate Subjects From Their Verbs

INCORRECT: Teenagers taking up smoking, often find it difficult to quit later in life, even in the face of health problems.

CORRECT: Teenagers taking up smoking often find it difficult to quit later in life, even in the face of health problems.

You can get away with separating a subject from its verb with an aside (and the two commas that go with it), but otherwise a subject and a verb form a complete idea that can't be split by a comma.

In the example above, *Teenagers taking up smoking* is the subject and *find* is the verb.

INCORRECT: Our family's having to spend the night at the hotel, was the last straw that motivated our father to buy an electric generator.

CORRECT: Our family's having to spend the night at the hotel was the last straw that motivated our father to buy an electric generator.

6. Don't Separate Compound Subjects, Predicates, or Objects

INCORRECT: The girls, and the boys had their own separate birthday parties.

CORRECT: The girls and the boys had their own separate birthday parties.

The girls and *the boys* are two individual elements of the compound subject, so they shouldn't be divided.

INCORRECT: Terrence ran to the restaurant, and met his father for lunch.

CORRECT: Terrence ran to the restaurant and met his father for lunch.

Ran to the restaurant and *met his father for lunch* are two elements of the compound predicate. Don't split them with a comma.

INCORRECT: I drove to the store, and the nail salon.

CORRECT: I drove to the store and the nail salon.

The store and *the nail salon* are both objects of the prepositional phrase starting with *to*. For that reason, they can't be separated by a comma.

---

7. Don't Separate an Independent Clause from the Dependent Clause That Follows

INCORRECT: He shined his shoes, while they waited.

CORRECT: He shined his shoes while they waited.

While they waited is a dependent clause. Therefore, it should not be separated from the independent clause with a comma.

INCORRECT: The child pushed all of the buttons in the elevator, when his mother told him he couldn't press any.

CORRECT: The child pushed all of the buttons in the elevator when his mother told him he couldn't press any.

The only exception to this rule is if there is a case in which the dependent clause creates an extreme contrast.

INCORRECT: The shopping addict maxed out her credit card although she'd had a $100,000 limit!

CORRECT: The shopping addict maxed out her credit card, although she'd had a $100,000 limit!

NOTES

_____

_____

_____

_____

_____

_____

_____

_____

_____

_____

_____

_____

_____

_____

_____

» WHAT SOUNDS WRONG IS WRONG

Most people have *heard* more correct English than they have *read*. Draw on this experience.

By quietly reading aloud to yourself, or by saying the lines silently in your head (also known as "The Secret Agent Move"), you can evaluate whether a choice "sounds wrong."

- **What sounds wrong is probably wrong.**

- Go with your gut.

- And **what sounds right is probably right.**

- If you aren't sure of the grammar rule, go with what sounds best and smoothest to you.

- **Don't be afraid to eliminate an answer choice that just sounds wrong.**

Likewise, listen for pauses in spoken English that indicate that a comma is necessary. In the example below, you can hear that choice G is incorrect because it does not sound natural to pause after *group*.

16. On <u>May 10th, 1869; a group</u> of government and railroad officials gathered to view the Driving of the Last Spike.

    F. NO CHANGE

    G. May 10, 1869, a group,

    H. May 10, 1869; a group,

    J. May 10, 1869, a group

PASSAGE III

Paul Cézanne: The Bridge Between Centuries

In the late 1800's, French painter Paul Cézanne (1839-1906) laid the foundation for the transition from 19th-century to 20th-century art. As with so many great artists, Cézanne
₃₀

were to be never fully appreciated until after his death.
₃₁

Therefore, throughout his lifetime, he was rejected and
₃₂

ridiculed by the artistic elite, but today he hails the bridge
₃₃
between the artistic movements of Impressionism and Cubism.

Born to wealthy parents in southern France, Cézanne enjoying a financial security unavailable to most struggling
₃₄
artists. In 1857, he began attending the Free Municipal School of Drawing in Aix-en-Provence. He devoted himself to his artistic career against the wishes of his father. Who
₃₅
did not reconcile with the young Cézanne until several years later.

In the arts, Cézanne went on to develop several
₃₆
foundational concepts of art. He was most fascinated by the simplification of natural objects to their basic geometric forms. He is quoted as saying that he wanted to "treat nature by the cylinder, the sphere, and the cone." These ideas would become the basis for Cubism. He utilized small, repetitive

---

30. The writer wants to suggest that Cézanne greatly influenced the evolution of art leading into the 20th century. Which choice best accomplishes that goal?
- **F.** NO CHANGE
- **G.** engaged in
- **H.** participated in
- **J.** contributed to

31. **A.** NO CHANGE
- **B.** if it were
- **C.** was
- **D.** if it was

32. **F.** NO CHANGE
- **G.** Because of this, throughout
- **H.** As a result, throughout
- **J.** Throughout

33. **A.** NO CHANGE
- **B.** is hailed as
- **C.** hailed
- **D.** is hail as

34. **F.** NO CHANGE
- **G.** enjoyed
- **H.** is enjoyed
- **J.** enjoys

35. **A.** NO CHANGE
- **B.** father; who
- **C.** father, who
- **D.** father, who,

36. **F.** NO CHANGE
- **G.** Pertaining to his artistic talent,
- **H.** On the subject of his art,
- **J.** DELETE the underlined portion

GO ON TO THE NEXT PAGE.

brush strokes and was interested in optics and complex points

of view. Many of his paintings, *Les Grandes Baigneuses*,
37
displays cylindrical trees bowing over nude figures on a

shore. It is noted as a triumph of stable geometric balance.
38

Despite his contributions to 20th century art, was greatly
39
underappreciated during his life, Cezanne's work. His works
39
were regularly rejected by the *Salon des Refusés*, an art

exhibition dedicated to works that had already been

rejected by the official Paris Salon. [40] Art critics ridiculed

his works when exhibited alongside the pieces of other
41
Impressionist painters.

The younger generation of artists, therefore, praised
42

37. A. NO CHANGE
   B. One
   C. Several
   D. More than one

38. If the underlined phrase were deleted, the sentence would primarily lose a detail that:
   F. repeats information found elsewhere in the sentence.
   G. is necessary for the sentence to be grammatically complete.
   H. provides new and relevant information.
   J. is ambiguous and unnecessary.

39. A. NO CHANGE
   B. 20th century art was greatly underappreciated during his life, despite his contributions to Cézanne's work.
   C. Despite his contributions to Cézanne's work, 20th century art was greatly underappreciated during his life.
   D. Despite his contributions to 20th century art, Cézanne's work was greatly underappreciated during his life.

40. The writer is considering adding the following phrase to the end of the preceding sentence (changing the period after *Salon* to a comma):

works by artists such as Camille Pissarro, Henri Fantin-Latour, and Édouard Manet.

Should the writer make this addition?

   F. Yes, because it offers relevant examples of Cezanne's contemporaries who were accepted by *Salon des Refusés.*
   G. Yes, because it helps explain what the Paris Salon is.
   H. No, because it provides a sampling of artists rather than a full listing.
   J. No, because it digresses from the topic being discussed in the paragraph.

41. A. NO CHANGE
   B. is
   C. were
   D. are

42. F. NO CHANGE
   G. however,
   H. because of this,
   J. additionally,

GO ON TO THE NEXT PAGE.

his work <u>than</u> revolutionary. Cézanne's work was not
₄₃

considered <u>Impressionist but as Post-Impressionist,</u> providing
₄₄
the precursor for a new age of artistic expression in the 20th

century. He inspired artists such as Braque, Metzinger, Gris,

and Picasso, and helped usher in a new paradigm for the

artistic world.

43. A. NO CHANGE
     B. as
     C. then
     D. so

44. F. NO CHANGE
     G. Impressionist; but as Post-Impressionist
     H. Impressionist but as, Post-Impressionist
     J. Impressionist, but as Post-Impressionist,

END OF TEST
STOP! DO NOT GO ON TO THE NEXT PAGE
UNTIL TOLD TO DO SO.

» SAY WHAT YOU MEAN

It's important that authors get their meaning across.

On the ACT, sometimes you'll need to help them out with this a bit.

- **The meaning of a phrase needs to be consistent with the rest of the sentence.**

- **The meaning of a sentence needs to be consistent with the paragraph.**

- **The best choice is clear and consistently meaningful.**

Look out for conjunctions, like "but" or "however," which indicate that what comes next contradicts what has already been stated.

Let's examine a practice question in order to see how this applies.

> **27.** <u>Before long,</u> books written in New York City could be found on shelves in San Francisco.
>
> A. NO CHANGE
>
> B. For instance,
>
> C. In example,
>
> D. That is,

The key to this question is that the other answer choices seem to indicate that this sentence is providing an example of what was said in the previous sentence, which talks about people and not about books at all. In this question, because of the *meaning* of the answer choices, only choice A makes sense.

Let's take a look at another one of the practice test questions:

> **28.** The writer wishes to add a sentence about the effect of the first Transcontinental Railroad on the United States' intellectual discourse. Given that all the following statements are true, which one, if added here, would most clearly and effectively accomplish the writer's goal?
>
> F. By bringing the western states firmly and profitably into the Union, the Transcontinental Railroad greatly improved the economic situation in the United States.
>
> G. The completion of the railroad allowed for the spreading of ideas throughout the United States at a much quicker pace.
>
> H. The railroad was built by three private companies.
>
> J. The first Transcontinental Railroad was commonly referred to as the Overland Route.

We have to make sure we choose the answer that most closely has the meaning being asked for in the question. Choice G mentions ideas, which are related to intellectual discourse, while no other answer gets close to doing so. Again, the *meaning* of the statement is what is being checked.

This concept of choosing the **clearest, most meaningful answer** is very important.

Let's take a look at one more practice question:

33. Throughout his lifetime, he was rejected and ridiculed often by the artistic elite, but today he <u>hails</u> the bridge between the artistic movements of Impressionism and Cubism.

A. NO CHANGE

B. is hailed as

C. hailed

D. is hail as

The first part of this sentence talks about Cézanne receiving rejection and criticism, so it doesn't make sense that the second part of the sentence talks about the artist's opinions about artistic movements. Choosing option B makes the sentence clearer and more consistent. Now both parts of the sentence are talking about Cézanne.

When in doubt, go for the answer that is clearest and provides the most consistent meaning.

NOTES

_____

_____

_____

_____

_____

_____

_____

_____

» SUBJECT, VERB, CAN WE AGREE?

- Subjects have a number (one or more than one) that must be matched by their verbs.

- In most circumstances, a subject and its verb can share only one "-s" between them.

- **Be sure you're comparing the actual subject to its verb.**

Often the ACT will interject prepositional phrases that insert an object of a preposition between a subject and verb.

Looking at the object instead of the subject can lead to choosing the incorrect verb number.

Let's see how this plays out in a practice question:

31. As with so many great artists, Cézanne <u>were to be</u> never fully appreciated until after his death.

A. NO CHANGE

B. if it were

C. was

D. if it was

If you get thrown off by the prepositional phrase *as with so many great artists*, you might mistake the object *artists* for the subject and want to choose a plural verb. The subject, however, is *Cézanne*, and, therefore, the singular *was* is the best choice.

» STRATEGIES FOR THE "BOX" QUESTIONS

See a number in a box? 40

These questions test your skills at organizing the passage and developing its main ideas.

- The key to "box" questions is to work for **consistency**.

- **Consistency means that something does not change.** It remains the same.

- You want to choose the option that flows best with what is already in the passage.

- Select the option that continues to develop the main idea already established.

- **Make sure you are answering the exact question being asked, not just selecting the answer that you like best.**

- It helps to read each answer choice, compare that to the question asked, and then work out what option best answers the question.

Look at this example:

40. The writer is thinking of adding the following phrase to the end of the preceding sentence (changing the period after *Salon* to a comma):

works by artists, such as Camille Pissarro, Henri Fantin-Latour, and Édouard Manet.

Should the writer make this addition?

F. Yes, because it offers relevant examples of Cezanne's contemporaries who were accepted by *Salon des Refusés.*

G. Yes, because it helps explain what the Paris Salon is.

H. No, because it provides a sampling of artists rather than a full listing.

J. No, because it digresses from the topic being discussed in the paragraph.

In this question, the addition of the phrase helps the reader to understand more about the *Salon des Refusés* and some of Cézanne's contemporaries. A full listing of the authors would be a digression, however, so eliminate choice H. Also, this phrase does not provide any information about the Paris Salon, itself, so choice G is an incorrect answer. This addition further develops the essay and is at least somewhat on point, so choice F is a better choice than choice J.

This page intentionally left blank.

PASSAGE IV

Friends for Life

[1]

[1] I met Will, my best friend to this day, sixteen years ago when his family moved into the house down the street. [2] I was seven years old. [3] We became inseparable

throughout our childhood, even though we always attended different schools.

[2]

Will was completely in love with video games and trading card games; I was more interested in reading books and skateboarding. Yet, we shared an appreciation for

one another's passions. More importantly though we just loved spending time together. We'd play games and go on adventures, and after so many years of being friends, we developed a rare connection.

[3]

Last December, Will and I were back in our hometown visiting our families. ☐49 Though it had been some time since we had seen or even spoken to one another, we knew with certainty that we would make time to meet while we were both in town. Will had been training in a linguistics program for the Air Force, while I was studying mathematics at Florida State University. We felt fortunate to be back in town at the same time.

[4]

I pulled into his parents' driveway at 9:30 a.m., carrying Will's Christmas gift. Will was staying in his old room at his parents' house for the holidays. It was wonderful to be back

45. How could these sentences be better arranged?
- A. NO CHANGE
- B. 2, 3, 1
- C. 2, 1, 3
- D. 3, 1, 2

46. F. NO CHANGE
- G. childhood; even
- H. childhood. Even
- J. childhood, even,

47. Which of the following alternatives to the underlined portion would NOT be acceptable?
- A. games. I
- B. games, I
- C. games, while I
- D. games. I, however,

48. F. NO CHANGE
- G. importantly, though
- H. importantly, though,
- J. important though

49. If the writer were to delete the preceding sentence, the essay would primarily lose:
- A. an explanation of the common interests that Will and the narrator shared.
- B. an explanation of what Will and the narrator had been doing for work.
- C. an explanation of how the narrator's friendship with Will had developed.
- D. an explanation of why Will and the narrator were in the same area.

GO ON TO THE NEXT PAGE.

in that house again after so long. It seemed that nothing had changed; the home held the same warmth that it always had. The same books stood near the mantel on the bookshelf in the living room. Will's mom,

whom had been in the kitchen making gumbo, answered the door with a huge smile on her face and hugged me.

[5]

Will was still in his pajamas. He greeted me with a smile. We hugged and exchanged greetings. It took us no

time at all to enter right back into the swing of our

timeless friendship. I gave him his Christmas present—

a rare foil trading card that he had been seeking for a long time. Inspecting it, he laughed and thanked me for the

gift, looking it over.

[6]

Us decided to play one of the trading card games he had taught me years ago. I didn't have any cards, but he had

50. **F.** NO CHANGE
    G. near the mantel in the living room on the bookshelf.
    H. on the bookshelf near the mantel in the living room.
    J. on the bookshelf in the living room near the mantel.

51. **A.** NO CHANGE
    B. who
    C. whose
    D. they

52. Which choice would best express Will's fond reaction to seeing the narrator for the first time after so long?
    F. NO CHANGE
    G. He yawned sleepily.
    H. He told me that he would go change quickly.
    J. He offered me a glass of water.

53. **A.** NO CHANGE
    B. come across
    C. drop by
    D. discover

54. Which of the following alternatives to the underlined portion would NOT be acceptable?
    F. enduring closeness
    G. lasting fondness
    H. momentary affection
    J. ageless bond

55. Which of the following alternatives to the underlined portion would NOT be acceptable?
    A. a scarcely
    B. an extraordinary
    C. a unique
    D. an uncommon

56. **F.** NO CHANGE
    G. gift, studying it intently.
    H. gift, taking its details.
    J. gift.

57. **A.** NO CHANGE
    B. We
    C. They
    D. Them

GO ON TO THE NEXT PAGE.

enough for the both of us. We joked and laughed throughout the entire game; of course, he beat me with ease. <u>After a while,</u> we realized that we were both hungry and decided to take a walk to Will's favorite restaurant in the area.
58

<u>We both felt glad that we were able to converse and behave like friends, despite the time we had spent apart.</u>
59

58. Which of the following alternatives to the underlined portion would NOT be acceptable?

    F. Eventually,
    G. At some point,
    H. Immediately,
    J. Later on,

59. Given that all the choices are true, which one would best conclude this essay by effectively summarizing its main idea?

    A. NO CHANGE
    B. It was clear to both of us that the years of separation had not affected our wonderful friendship at all.
    C. We were sad to realize that, as we were beginning our professional lives, we would have fewer and fewer of these moments.
    D. It was a bittersweet thing; we knew that our friendship was strong, but bound to fade over time.

Question 60 asks about the preceding passage as a whole.

---

60. Upon reviewing the essay and finding that some information has been left out, the writer composes the following sentence incorporating that information:

With so much school work, both of our lives had become incredibly busy.

This sentence would most logically be placed:

    F. at the beginning of paragraph 4.
    G. after sentence 1 in paragraph 3.
    H. after sentence 3 in paragraph 3.
    J. at the end of paragraph 5.

END OF TEST
STOP! DO NOT GO ON TO THE NEXT PAGE
UNTIL TOLD TO DO SO.

This page intentionally left blank.

» QUESTIONS OVER THE ANSWER CHOICES

Let's look over this question from the mini-test:

52. Which choice would best express Will's fond reaction to seeing the narrator for the first time after so long?

F. NO CHANGE

G. He yawned sleepily.

H. He told me that he would go change quickly.

J. He offered me a glass of water.

When you see a specific question above the answer choices, remember that the question takes precedence. It's boss!

You're no longer looking for the best choice for the passage or the choice that's grammatically correct.

• **Identify the answer that *absolutely fits the question*—not necessarily the answer choice that works best with the rest of the passage.**

In the case of this example, only choice F clearly indicates that Will has a positive emotion toward the narrator (a smile). Yawning, changing quickly, and water are not necessarily friendly reactions! Don't let yourself overthink it.

NOTES

_____

_____

_____

_____

_____

_____

_____

This page intentionally left blank.

PASSAGE V

Three Mythical Rivers

Throughout human history, people of various cultures and religions around the world have developed their own stories regarding rivers. These may be tales of spirits or
61

magical creatures, residing within the waters or some
62
mythical characteristics attributed to a particular river. Among these stories, the variety and kind are numerous, with each society creating myths, or legends, specific to its own
63
ways of life. However,

their is one motif in particular that pervades many
64
mythologies developed by the religions of the world:

the river separating life from the afterlife.
65

Likely the most famous example is the River Styx,
66
which means "hate" in Ancient Greek. According to Greek mythology, the underworld, also known as Hades, was circled nine times by the River Styx. In ancient Greek

funerals, it was customary to leave coins in the mouths of
67

61. A. NO CHANGE
　　B. stories to
　　C. stories which they connected to
　　D. stories, related to

62. F. NO CHANGE
　　G. creatures residing
　　H. creatures, residing,
　　J. creatures residing,

63. A. NO CHANGE
　　B. myths, or legends
　　C. myths, or legends:
　　D. myths, or legends;

64. F. NO CHANGE
　　G. they're
　　H. there
　　J. but there

65. Given that all the choices are true, which one ends this paragraph with the clearest allusion to the quality demonstrated by all the rivers described later in the essay?

　　A. NO CHANGE
　　B. named for hate, pain, and sin.
　　C. requiring a payment of coins for crossing.
　　D. appearing as blood to some and nectar to others.

66. Given that all the choices are true, which one offers visual information about the River Styx?

　　F. NO CHANGE
　　G. The waterway feared by the gods, spiraling around the underworld,
　　H. Likely an example that is chilling to readers
　　J. The mythological river that has been most studied by modern day scholars

67. Given that all the choices are true, which one provides a detail that has the most direct connection to the information that follows in this sentence?

　　A. NO CHANGE
　　B. convenient
　　C. obvious
　　D. a good idea

GO ON TO THE NEXT PAGE.

the deceased. Those who passed without this coin would not
68
be able to pay the ferryman, Charon, the fee required to carry

them across the water. They would be left on the shores of

the River Styx eternally, never able to cross into the afterlife.

In ancient Japanese mythology, the Sanzu River, or the

River of Three Crossings, holding striking similarities to
69

the River Styx. Developed from Japanese Buddhist religious
70
belief, the myth told that in order to reach the afterlife, all
70
souls were required to cross the river. The deceased were

buried with six coins in their caskets. Based on the life the

deceased had lived, crossing the river could be very simple

or exceedingly difficult. I think it's really crazy, children who
71
died before their parents were confined to the riverbed of

the Sanzu, where they were made to build towers of pebbles

continuously until entering the safety of the afterlife.

In ancient Hindu religious texts, the myth, of the
72
Vaitarna River is told. The river is said to lie between the
72
earth and the infernal Naraka, the realm of Yama, Hindu God

of Death. In the myth of the Vaitarna River, only those who

sinned were required to cross the river, so the righteous saw it
73
as a cleansing river of nectar, the sinner saw it as a river of

blood. Frightening and terrible in appearance, and the river
74
could be crossed in many ways. If the sinner could not cross

the river, however, he or she would be stranded on the shores

68. Which of the following alternatives to the underlined portion would NOT be acceptable?
  F. the departed
  G. the dead
  H. the perished
  J. the subsisting

69. A. NO CHANGE
  B. hold
  C. having held
  D. holds

70. F. NO CHANGE
  G. the Japanese,
  H. Japan,
  J. Japanese,

71. A. NO CHANGE
  B. I find it odd, children
  C. It is bizarre, children
  D. Children

72. F. NO CHANGE
  G. the myth, of the Vaitarna River,
  H. the myth of the Vaitarna River,
  J. the myth of the Vaitarna River

73. A. NO CHANGE
  B. because
  C. and while
  D. after

74. F. NO CHANGE
  G. appearance, the
  H. appearance, the,
  J. appearance; the

GO ON TO THE NEXT PAGE.

of the Vaitarna forever, unable to be reborn. [75]

75. The writer is considering adding the following phrase to the end of this paragraph:

The mythology around the Vaitarna River in Hindu culture is the most interesting because it is not only the sinners who have to travel the river to get to the afterlife.

Would this addition be an appropriate conclusion to the passage as a whole?

A. Yes, because it offers additional information about the Vaitarna River.

B. Yes, because it talks about everyone who has to cross the river, good or bad.

C. No, because Greek culture also requires the righteous to cross the River Styx.

D. No, because it is too specific to one of the three cultures to be a conclusion to the entire passage.

END OF TEST
STOP! DO NOT GO ON TO THE NEXT PAGE
UNTIL TOLD TO DO SO.

This page intentionally left blank.

» ENGLISH WRAP-UP

The English test is always the first section of the ACT.

By preparing thoroughly for the challenge, you can start on the right foot on test day.

If you would like further practice on the ACT English test, check out these recommended resources:

ACT English Mini-Tests on page 198

Mastery for the ACT English

SnapCourse for the ACT English

The Elements of Style by Strunk & White

Elements of Grammar by Margaret Shertzer

Grammar Girl Presents the Ultimate Writing Guide for Students by Mignon Fogarty

NOTES

_____

_____

_____

_____

_____

_____

_____

_____

_____

_____

_____

_____

» ANSWER EXPLANATIONS FOR ENGLISH PRACTICE TEST

1. **The correct answer is B.** The comma in this sentence is needed to separate the independent clause from the compound participle phrase modifying it. The other choices use commas incorrectly by creating either a comma splice or a list structure where it is not appropriate.

2. **The correct answer is F.** The sentence correctly makes use of an em dash to show a parenthetical statement or interruption. Choices G and J incorrectly use semicolons, and choice H creates a run-on sentence.

3. **The correct answer is D.** Using the pronoun *they* creates the question of an ambiguous antecedent, making it seem that *they* may be replacing *the city*. Replace this pronoun with *people* to make the sentence clearer.

4. **The correct answer is J.** Choices F, G, and H are all acceptable answers and are therefore not the correct choices since question 4 is looking for an alternative that is NOT acceptable. Choice J is not acceptable because the past participle version of routine (routined) does not fit and makes the sentence incoherent.

5. **The correct answer is D.** Choice A leaves a comma splice. Choice D correctly uses the conjunction *and* to connect the two independent clauses.

6. **The correct answer is G.** This sentence explains what the narrator is ready to do on the beach—*walk farther than I ever have before.* Therefore, this sentence helps the reader understand what the narrator intends to do on the beach.

7. **The correct answer is D.** Choices A, B, and C all have negative connotations. Choice D is the only one that has a positive, peaceful connotation. If the definition of *tranquil* is unclear, use the process of elimination to determine that *crippled*, *somber*, and *decrepit* imply a slow, crawling drag, which is not consistent with the tone of the passage. Thus, the fourth option, *tranquil*, must be the correct choice.

8. **The correct answer is F.** The passage is written in first person. Choice G is incorrect because it switches to second person. Choice H is incorrect because it switches to third person. Choice J creates an incomplete sentence. Choice F is the only option that maintains consistency.

9. **The correct answer is C.** In the phrase *slipping quietly*, the word *quietly* is an adverb describing *slipping*. These should not be separated by a comma. Likewise, the phrase should not be separated by a semicolon from the rest of the sentence as seen in choice D. The only option with correct punctuation is choice C.

10. **The correct answer is F.** Choice F is grammatically correct and more concise than the other choices. Although each of the other choices are also grammatically correct, they are less concise and do not offer any additional information to the passage. Additionally, the structure of this choice is more consistent with what came before in the paragraph.

11. **The correct answer is A.** The other answer choices do not make sense in the context of the dependent clause: *assaulting the quiet shore with steps that splash.* Choice A effectively introduces a contrast between the narrator's leisurely walk and the pair of runners who whip by.

12. The correct answer is J. Choices F, G, and H all create a run-on sentence because two independent clauses must be separated by a period, semicolon, or comma and conjunction. Each of these answer options is incorrect because a comma alone, no punctuation at all, or a conjunction alone cannot join two independent clauses. Only choice J correctly places a period between the two clauses.

13. The correct answer is A. Choice B creates a run-on sentence. Choice D needlessly misuses a colon. Choice C incorrectly uses a comma and the conjunction *and* to separate two clauses. Choice A is the only option to correctly join the introductory phrase *spending hours walking* with the independent clause that follows it.

14. The correct answer is F. The word *lawns* is not possessive in this sentence, so choices G, H, and J are all incorrect.

15. The correct answer is B. The essay devotes a great deal of its content to providing images and examples of the peaceful atmosphere of the beach and the narrator's enjoyment of this atmosphere. The other answers have information that is either irrelevant or never mentioned.

16. The correct answer is J. Choices F and H incorrectly use semicolons. Choice G incorrectly separates a noun from the prepositional phrase modifying it. Choice J correctly uses commas to offset *1869* and uses no additional unnecessary punctuation.

17. The correct answer is C. Choice A incorrectly uses a semicolon. Choice B incorrectly uses a comma to separate *the* from the phrase following it. Choice D creates a run-on sentence. Choice C correctly uses a colon, beginning the sentence with an independent clause and supplying a description of the clause after the colon.

18. The correct answer is G. Choice G correctly uses the adjective, *ceremonial*, to modify the gerund, *driving*. Choices F and J use incorrect noun and adverb forms of the root word, *ceremony*, respectively. Choice H incorrectly places a comma between noun and gerund.

19. The correct answer is C. By including this phrase in the sentence, the amount of preparation necessary for the construction of the railroad is made clear. *Exploration and planning* are definitely part of preparation. Choices A and B are partially correct but not completely accurate, since *a decade of exploration and planning* does not really tell us about costs or difficulties. Choice D can be eliminated because this sentence is discussing what happened before construction, not its resulting effects.

20. The correct answer is H. Choices F and J incorrectly use colons with the preposition *as*. Choice G incorrectly uses a comma to separate a prepositional phrase from the phrase it is modifying. Choice H is correct because there is no punctuation required before the prepositional phrase modifying *were employed*.

21. The correct answer is A. *Required for efficient construction* is the most meaningful choice of those provided. The other choices do not provide specific information regarding the construction and are less concise.

22. The correct answer is J. Deleting the underlined portion removes redundant information. It is already clear that the construction took six years to complete based on the phrase *beginning in 1863 and finishing in 1869*.

23. The correct answer is C. Choices A and B incorrectly use plural pronouns to replace the singular noun *event*. Choice D assumes the antecedent is *man*. Choice C provides the proper pronoun, *it*, for the singular noun *event*.

24. The correct answer is J. No commas should be used to separate the preposition *at Promontory Summit* from the noun it modifies, *crowd*. Choice F unnecessarily separates the preposition from the noun. Choice H tries to make the prepositional phrase an aside by surrounding it in commas, but the phrase is too essential to the meaning of the sentence for this to work. Choice G incorrectly uses an em dash to set off crucial information. An em dash can be used to denote that what comes next is an aside or parenthetical statement, and it is incorrect for the same reason that the comma used in choice F is incorrect.

25. The correct answer is A. Choice A is concise and does not leave out any vital information. Choices B and C are grammatically correct but are too long-winded without providing additional information. Choice D, however, would remove vital and new information, so it is likewise incorrect.

26. The correct answer is G. By selecting the pronoun *whom* as the object of the prepositional phrase *many of whom*, you tightly link the second clause to modifying the first clause and prevent the sentence from becoming a run-on. The subjective form of the pronoun *who* is an incorrect choice because it's being used as the object of a preposition.

27. The correct answer is A. *Before long* is the best transition for this sentence. It implies a gradual change brought about by the completion of the railroad. *For instance* and *for example* both imply that an example of something will be provided. *That is* implies that a restatement of a previous statement will be provided.

28. The correct answer is G. Choice G is the only answer that is relevant to the *intellectual discourse* of the United States. Choices F, H, and J are all related to the railroad but are not relevant to the question asked. Although another choice might be well-suited as a concluding statement for the passage, it is important that the chosen answer is the best fit for the specific question.

29. The correct answer is C. The sentence should appear in the description of the *Driving of the Last Spike* event. Paragraphs should be organized in such a way that all related content goes into the same paragraph or nearby paragraphs.

30. The correct answer is F. Choices G, H, and J all imply that Cézanne simply made some contribution to the evolution of art leading into the 20th century. However, choice F implies that he was a key figure in this evolution, greatly influencing it, since *foundation* here means "the beginning and principles" for *the transition from 19th-century to 20th-century art*.

31. The correct answer is C. Cézanne is a singular proper noun, requiring a singular verb. Choice A provides a plural verb. Choices B and D provide conditional verbs that do not make sense in the sentence.

32. The correct answer is J. Choices F, G, and H all provide transitions that imply the sentence is true because of what is said in the preceding sentence. However, this is not the case. Just because Cézanne was *never completely appreciated* does not automatically mean that he was *rejected and ridiculed*, so it is best to delete the underlined portion altogether.

33. The correct answer is B. Choices A and C are incorrect verb forms as they imply that Cézanne is the subject who is hailing. Choice D is an incorrect conjugation of the word *hail*. Choice B is the correct answer because it provides the correct form of the verb, which implies that Cézanne is being hailed by others.

34. The correct answer is G. Throughout the passage, the author speaks about Cézanne in the past tense. Choices F, H, and J provide incorrect verb forms and inconsistent tenses. Choice G provides the correct form of the verb in past tense.

35. The correct answer is C. Choice A creates an incomplete sentence. Choice B incorrectly uses a semicolon to separate an independent clause from a dependent clause. Choice D incorrectly uses a comma to separate *who* from the rest of the clause. Choice C correctly uses a single comma to separate an independent clause from a nonessential clause that provides additional information about Cézanne's father.

36. The correct answer is J. Choices F, G, and H are redundant. Therefore, the underlined portion can be deleted.

37. The correct answer is B. This particular sentence is referring to a specific painting by Cézanne, *Les Grandes Baigneuses*. Choices A, C, and D all imply that there are several paintings being discussed. Furthermore, a singular pronoun is required to match the singular verb *displays*.

38. The correct answer is H. Although this information is not vital to the understanding of the sentence, it is neither irrelevant nor redundant. Choices F and J are incorrect for this reason. Choice G is incorrect because the sentence would still be grammatically correct if the underlined portion were missing.

39. The correct answer is D. This is the clearest, easiest-to-read choice (not to mention the most grammatically correct!). All things being equal, go with the choice that most clearly communicates the idea the author is trying to get across without making you tongue-tied trying to read it!

40. The correct answer is F. The addition provides examples to help the reader understand the types of artists being described. Choice G is incorrect because the addition does not describe anything about the Paris Salon. Choice H is incorrect because it would be irrelevant to list all of the artists who were rejected from the Paris Salon. Choice J is incorrect because the addition pertains to the topic of the paragraph.

41. The correct answer is A. Choices B, C, and D are verbs and do not make sense in the sentence. Choice C properly includes a conjunction that relates the first part of the sentence to the second part of the sentence.

42. The correct answer is G. Choices F and H imply that the information in the sentence is a result of the preceding sentence, but this is not the case. Choice J implies that the information is in accordance with the information in the previous sentence. Only choice G correctly implies that the information in the sentence is in contrast to the information in the previous sentence.

43. The correct answer is B. Choices A, C, and D utilize conjunctions and do not make sense in the sentence. Choice B, using the adverb *as*, is the only choice that allows the sentence to make sense, communicating that the artists thought his work was *revolutionary*.

44. The correct answer is J. A comma is needed after *Impressionist* in order to completely set off the phrase *but as Post-Impressionist* from the prior clause and the participle phrase following it. Choice H incorrectly separates the adverb from the rest of its phrase. Choice G incorrectly uses a semicolon since the second part of the sentence cannot stand on its own.

45. The correct answer is A. Choice A presents the information logically: introducing that the paragraph is about the narrator's relationship with his best friend, giving context, and finally transitioning into the rest of the passage. Choices B, C, and D make the paragraph feel out of sequence.

46. The correct answer is F. Choice G incorrectly uses a semicolon, since the second part of the sentence is a dependent clause. Choice H creates an incomplete sentence. Choice J incorrectly uses a comma to interrupt the phrase *even though*.

47. The correct answer is B. Choice B creates a comma splice, making it the only incorrect answer choice. The instructions require choosing the unacceptable answer.

48. The correct answer is H. The word *though* is a parenthetical element and should be set off with commas. Choices F and G incorrectly use a single comma. Choice J makes the sentence unclear, as it doesn't clarify how *though* is functioning in the sentence.

49. The correct answer is D. Choices A, B, and C are all incorrect because they reference either incorrect or irrelevant information. The author says, *Will and I were back in our old hometown visiting our families*, which provides an explanation of why they were once more in the same area.

50. The correct answer is H. Choice H makes it clear that the books are on the bookshelf, the bookshelf is near the mantel, and the mantel is in the living room. Choices F, G, and J utilize orders that make it unclear where these objects are located with respect to each other. Choice H is also the most fluent (the others sound like we're playing a game of Clue!).

51. The correct answer is B. Choices A, C, and D are all pronouns that are incorrect for this sentence. *Whom* is incorrect because the pronoun is being used as a subject, not an object. *Whose* is possessive and, therefore, incorrectly used. *They* is a plural pronoun that doesn't match its singular antecedent, *mom*. Choice B uses *who*, which is the correct subjective form of the pronoun, so this choice is correct.

52. The correct answer is F. Choices G, H and J all demonstrate either apathy or nonchalance toward the narrator. Choice F shows warmth and kindness toward the narrator. Will's smile is the best choice that demonstrates his *fond reaction*.

53. The correct answer is A. Choices B, C, and D all suggest a sort of surprising discovery. The tone of the passage and the sentence would better suggest a seamless entry into the narrator and his friend's old ways. For that reason, choice A is best.

54. The correct answer is H. Choices F, G, and J all provide phrases that are synonymous with the phrase *timeless friendship*. In choice H, the word *affection* can effectively be synonymous with the word *friendship*; however, *momentary* is an antonym for *timeless*. Choice H is the only incorrect choice.

55. The correct answer is A. Each of the provided choices are synonymous with the word *rare*. However, choice A provides the adverb form *scarcely* as opposed to the adjective form *scarce*. Because the sentence calls for an adjective, choice A is the only incorrect choice.

56. The correct answer is J. Choices F, G, and H all provide redundant information. These choices are synonymous with the phrase *inspecting it*, which appears at the beginning of the sentence. Therefore, choice J is correct; it is best to remove the underlined portion and end the sentence with a period after *gift*.

57. The correct answer is B. Choices A and D provide pronouns that are used only as objects. Choice C provides a third-person pronoun and is not consistent with the rest of the passage, since the subject is the narrator and his friend. Choice B provides a first-person plural pronoun used as a subject, so this is the best answer.

58. The correct answer is H. Choices F, G, and J are synonymous with the phrase *after a while*. However, choice H is contrary to this phrase, making it the only incorrect answer. Also, the choice *immediately* indicates that what happened in the sentence occurred right away, but this is not consistent with the information in the paragraph (since the two had time to play an *entire game*).

59. The correct answer is B. The essay describes how the two friends have remained close regardless of their growth in age and distance. Because the passage is upbeat about the relationship between the narrator and his friend, choice B appears to be the best choice. Choices A, C, and D may be accurate or grammatically correct, but they do not best fit the passage and its tone. These choices do not convey the overall idea of the passage as clearly as choice B does.

60. The correct answer is H. Paragraph 3 speaks largely about the current whereabouts and activities of the narrator and his friend. This sentence is best placed after sentence 3 in paragraph 3 because it describes how busy the two had become after beginning their respective studies. Placing the sentence before their new educational activities are mentioned makes it seem abrupt and out of place, so G is not the best choice.

61. The correct answer is A. Choice B does not make sense in the context of the sentence. Choice C is grammatically incorrect without commas to offset the parenthetical phrase. Choice D incorrectly uses a comma to separate a participle from the noun it modifies, *stories*. Choice A is the only grammatically correct answer.

62. The correct answer is G. Choices F, H, and J all incorrectly use commas. Choice G is the only correct answer, as there is no punctuation necessary for the sentence to be grammatically correct. The participle does not need to be separated from its modifier.

63. The correct answer is A. The phrase *or legends* is a parenthetical phrase providing further meaning to the word *myths* and should be properly offset by a pair of commas. Choice B incorrectly uses a single comma. Choice C incorrectly uses a colon to interrupt the sentence. Choice D incorrectly uses a semicolon; the second part of the sentence is not an independent clause, which makes choice A the correct answer.

64. The correct answer is H. Choice F shows possession. Choice G is a contraction of *they are*. Choice J incorrectly includes an unnecessary conjunction. Choice H is the only correct choice, as it is the only one that utilizes the proper version of *there* for establishing the existence of something.

65. The correct answer is A. Choice A is a proper description of all of the mythological rivers mentioned in the passage, since they have ties to each culture's afterlife mythology. Choice B describes only the River Styx. Choice C describes only the River Styx and the Sanzu River. Choice D describes only the Vaitarna River.

66. The correct answer is G. The choice that offers the most visual information regarding the River Styx is choice G. While choices F, H, and J all offer relevant and accurate information regarding the mythological river, choice G is the only one that is particularly visual in nature.

67. **The correct answer is A.** From the context of the sentence, choice A has the most direct connection to the sentence. Because the sentence describes the customs of ancient Greek funerals, the word *customary* seems to be the best choice.

68. **The correct answer is J.** Choices F, G, and H all provide synonyms for *the deceased*. However, since choice J offers an antonym, it is the only incorrect answer. If the reader is uncertain what the word *subsisting* means, the process of elimination should be used.

69. **The correct answer is D.** *The Sanzu River*, a singular proper noun, is the subject of the sentence and requires a singular action verb. Choices A and C cause the sentence to be incomplete. Choice B is a plural verb. Choice D causes the subject and verb to agree, so it is the correct choice.

70. **The correct answer is F.** Choice F provides additional and relevant information without being redundant. While choices G and H are technically accurate, they do not provide as much information as choice F.

71. **The correct answer is D.** Choices A and B use informal speech in an otherwise formal passage. Choice C is grammatically incorrect. Omitting the introductory phrase and beginning the sentence with *children* is the safest choice and maintains the tone of the passage, which makes choice D the correct answer.

72. **The correct answer is J.** Choices F, G, and H incorrectly use commas. Choice J is the only correct answer, as there is no punctuation necessary for the sentence to be grammatically correct. You can't insert a comma between a noun and the preposition that modifies it.

73. **The correct answer is C.** Choice A incorrectly suggests that the first clause implies the second clause. Choice B incorrectly insinuates that the second clause implies the first clause. Choice D incorrectly implies a chronological order to the clauses. Choice C is the best answer as it correctly shows the non-causal relationship between the two clauses without drawing incorrect conclusions between them.

74. **The correct answer is G.** *Frightening and terrible in appearance* is a phrase modifying *the river*, so it should be separated from the sentence with a comma. No conjunction is necessary after the comma because the phrase modifies the noun that comes right after it.

75. **The correct answer is D.** The entire passage is comparing the similarities between the three cultures and their lore. The sentence the writer is considering adding only mentions one of the rivers and, therefore, would not be a fitting conclusion to this passage as a whole.

SECTION THREE
Math

» INTRODUCTION TO THE ACT MATH TEST

- The ACT Math test consists of **60 questions**, which you must answer in **60 minutes**.

- Most people think of complicated trigonometry when they think of ACT math, but the truth is that **your score is mainly determined by your ability to solve word problems and your skill and accuracy in pre-algebra, algebra, and geometry.**

- You could get a 33 on the ACT Math test without knowing any trig.

- In this section, we'll work on improving your speed and accuracy in math.

- We'll also cover the content that most students miss to help you pick up an extra point or two on the test.

- You will need to know the following formulas for the test:

Area of a Square: $A = s^2$

Area of a Rectangle: $A = lw$

Area of a Triangle: $A = \frac{1}{2} bh$

Area of a Circle: $A = \pi r^2$

Area of a Parallelogram: $A = bh$

Area of a Trapezoid: $A = \frac{b_1 + b_2}{2} h$

Circumference of a Circle: $C = 2\pi r$

Volume of a Cube: $V = s^3$

Volume of a Rectangular Prism: $V = lwh$

Volume of a Cylinder: $V = \pi r^2 h$

Pythagorean Theorem: $c^2 = a^2 + b^2$

Equation of a Line: $y = mx + b$

Equation of a Circle: $(x - h)^2 + (y - k)^2 = r^2$

Sine: $\sin \theta = \frac{\text{opposite}}{\text{hypotenuse}}$

Cosine: $\cos \theta = \frac{\text{adjacent}}{\text{hypotenuse}}$

Tangent: $\tan \theta = \frac{\text{opposite}}{\text{adjacent}}$

Cosecant: $\csc \theta = \frac{\text{hypotenuse}}{\text{opposite}}$

Secant: $\sec \theta = \frac{\text{hypotenuse}}{\text{adjacent}}$

Cotangent: $\cot \theta = \frac{\text{adjacent}}{\text{opposite}}$

- You will NOT need to know the following formulas for the test:

Volume of a Sphere

Volume of a Cone

Volume of a Pyramid

Surface Area of a Sphere

Law of Cosines

Law of Sines

» SPEED UP OR SLOW DOWN?

The key to doing well on the math test is to **choose the right pacing strategy** based on **your goal score**.

What is your goal score for the math test? _____

If your goal score is **a 24 or above**, you should make use of the **Math Blitz** pacing method explained on page 70.

If your goal score is **below a 24**, you should make use of the **Cherry-Picking** pacing method explained on page 71.

Which pacing method will you use on the math test? _____

NOTES

_____

_____

_____

_____

_____

_____

_____

_____

_____

_____

_____

_____

_____

_____

_____

» HOW TO GET 10 EXTRA MINUTES

How much would your score improve if you had an extra 10 minutes on the ACT Math section?

By pacing yourself and by practicing in order to improve your speed, **you can grab an extra 10 minutes** or more for the tougher questions toward the end of the test.

- You want to blitz the first 20 questions, moving through them in only 10 minutes.

- Allow yourself 20 minutes for the middle 20 questions.

- Then you'll have a full 30 minutes for the last 20 questions.

There are some "gimmies" at the back of the test that you'll miss if you never get to them.

By working through the practice tests in this Boot Camp at the correct pace, you'll take a big step toward achieving better timing on the ACT.

NOTES

_____

_____

_____

_____

_____

_____

_____

_____

_____

_____

_____

_____

_____

» CHERRY-PICKING

Have you ever made simple mistakes on the easier questions in the beginning because you were rushing them? Did you end up missing the tougher questions at the end anyway?

By slowing down on the earlier questions and by taking more guesses on the tougher ones, **you can improve your accuracy** on the questions you know how to answer.

- If you know how to solve a question, take the time to show your work and answer it.

- If you are unable to answer a question, make your best guess and then mark and move.

- It helps to set a goal; look at how many questions you need for your scale score and attempt 5 more than that on your math test.

Rushing the questions you know how to do only to get stuck on questions you can't answer is not a good strategy. **By targeting the questions you can answer in the practice tests in this book and taking your time with them, you will improve your accuracy and manage your time better on the ACT.**

NOTES

_____

_____

_____

_____

_____

_____

_____

_____

_____

_____

_____

_____

MATHEMATICS TEST
60 Minutes — 60 Questions

DIRECTIONS: Begin by working out each problem. Once solved, choose the correct answer, then fill in its corresponding bubble on your answer sheet.

Do not waste time on difficult questions. Instead, leave them for last; by answering as many questions as possible first, you can use any remaining time to return to the others.

A calculator is allowed for any problems you choose, but some may be better solved without one.

Note: Unless stated otherwise, the following should be assumed:

1. Illustrative figures are NOT necessarily drawn to scale.
2. Geometric figures lie on the *x,y* coordinate plane.
3. The word "line" indicates a straight line.
4. The word "average" indicates a calculated mean.

---

1. Printer A can print 30 pages per minute. Printer B can print 40 pages per minute. Printer B begins printing 3 minutes after Printer A begins printing. Both printers stop printing 10 minutes after Printer A started. Together, how many pages did the two printers print?

   A. 120
   B. 580
   C. 610
   D. 700
   E. 1,200

2. The expression $(5x + 3y^2)(5x - 3y^2)$ is equivalent to:

   F. $10x^2 + 6y^4$
   G. $25x^2 + 9y^4$
   H. $10x^2 - 6y^4$
   J. $25x^2 - 9y^4$
   K. $25x^2 - 6y^4$

3. If $7(x - 7) = -15$, then $x = ?$

   A. $-\dfrac{64}{7}$

   B. $-\dfrac{34}{7}$

   C. $-\dfrac{15}{7}$

   D. $\dfrac{34}{7}$

   E. $\dfrac{64}{7}$

4. The daily fee for admission to the Florida Fun 'n Sun Amusement Park is $45 per adult and $25 per child. Daily admission fees are paid for a adults and c children. Which of the following expressions gives the total amount, in dollars, collected for daily fees?

   F. $45a + 25c$
   G. $45c + 25a$
   H. $25(a + c)$
   J. $70(a + c)$
   K. $25(a + c) + 45a$

5. Natalie makes $9.50 per hour for up to 40 hours a week working at a local bookstore. She is paid an overtime wage of 1.5 times her regular pay for every hour she works over 40 hours. If Natalie works 43 hours in a week, how much will she make that week?

   A. $380.00
   B. $394.25
   C. $408.50
   D. $422.00
   E. $422.75

6. Discounted tickets to the cinema cost $6.00 each. James spent $72.00 on discounted tickets, $54.00 less than he would have spent if he had bought tickets without the discount. What is the price of a ticket without a discount?

   F. $ 6.00
   G. $ 6.50
   H. $10.50
   J. $12.00
   K. $16.50

7. Which of the following mathematical expressions is equivalent to the verbal expression "A number, y, cubed is 42 more than the product of 13 and y"?

   A. $3y = 42 + 13y$
   B. $3y = 42y + 13y$
   C. $y^3 = 42 - 13y$
   D. $y^3 = 42 + y^{13}$
   E. $y^3 = 42 + 13y$

8. A rectangle has a perimeter of 24 meters and an area of 35 square meters. What is the length, in meters, of the longer side?

   F. 1
   G. 3
   H. 5
   J. 7
   K. 8

GO ON TO THE NEXT PAGE.

9. If $k = 7$, $j = 4$, and $p = -5$, what does $(k+j)(k+p-j)$ equal?

   A. −22
   B. 0
   C. 22
   D. 44
   E. 88

10. Jason's class projects are graded on a scale of 250 points. Jason has received scores of 245, 215, 220, and 224 for his first four projects. Jason worked out his average score on his projects thus far. In order to maintain the same average grade on projects, what grade must Jason receive on his 5th and final class project?

    F. 200
    G. 215
    H. 224
    J. 226
    K. 245

11. For 2 consecutive integers, the result of adding the smaller integer and four times the larger integer is 84. What are the 2 integers?

    A. 15,16
    B. 16,17
    C. 17,18
    D. 18,19
    E. 19,20

12. If $4^x = 52$, then which of the following must be true?

    F. $1 < x < 2$
    G. $2 < x < 3$
    H. $3 < x < 4$
    J. $4 < x < 5$
    K. $x > 5$

13. In $\triangle ABC$, the sum of the measures of $\angle A$ and $\angle B$ is 66°. What is the measure of $\angle C$?

    A. 57°
    B. 66°
    C. 90°
    D. 114°
    E. 124°

14. A function $f(x)$ is defined as $f(x) = -7x^2$. What is $f(-2)$?

    F. −121
    G. −28
    H. 28
    J. 98
    K. 121

15. At an ice cream parlor, patrons make their own sundaes from 5 flavors of ice cream, 2 sauces, 4 toppings, and 3 fruits. How many different sundaes can be made by a patron who chooses exactly 1 ice cream flavor, 1 sauce, 1 topping, and 1 fruit?

    A. 14
    B. 24
    C. 60
    D. 64
    E. 120

16. The base of a triangle is four times the base of a smaller triangle. The two triangles have the same height. The area of the smaller triangle is A square units. The area of the larger triangle is kA square units. Which of the following is the value of k?

    F. $\frac{1}{4}$

    G. $\frac{1}{2}$

    H. 1

    J. 2

    K. 4

17. What is the least common multiple of 30, 40, and 70?

    A. 84
    B. 120
    C. 840
    D. 1,200
    E. 84,000

18. The bacteria population of a nutrient broth grows according to the equation $y = 21(3)^t$, where t represents time in days and y represents the population. According to this equation, which answer will represent the bacteria population of the nutrient broth after 5 days?

    F. 63
    G. 315
    H. 1,701
    J. 5,103
    K. 15,309

GO ON TO THE NEXT PAGE.

19. Mind Beats Audio is designing a box for its new line of professional headphones. The box is a rectangular prism that is 28 centimeters long, 19 centimeters wide, and has a volume of 6,384 cubic centimeters. What is the height, in centimeters, of the box?

   A. 10
   B. 12
   C. 19
   D. 48
   E. 63

20. Four points, *L*, *M*, *N*, and *P*, lie on a circle with a circumference of 18 units. Point *M* is 4 units counterclockwise from point *L*. Point *N* is 6 units clockwise from point *L*. Point *P* is 9 units counterclockwise from point *L* and 9 units clockwise from point *L*. Moving clockwise and starting with point *L*, in what order are the points arranged?

   F. *L, M, N, P*
   G. *L, M, P, N*
   H. *L, P, M, N*
   J. *L, N, M, P*
   K. *L, N, P, M*

END OF TEST
STOP! DO NOT GO ON TO THE NEXT PAGE
UNTIL TOLD TO DO SO.

This page intentionally left blank.

» FUNCTIONS ARE YOUR FRIENDS

The secret to solving a function problem is taking your time.

Don't rush! It's easy to mess up a negative sign or be inaccurate with your arithmetic.

Plug in the number that appears inside of the parentheses in place of *x* in the equation.

Keep parentheses around this number when you plug it in until you actually start doing operations.

This way it's more difficult to make an error.

Let's take a look at how taking the time to be accurate can save you a point on the ACT.

14. A function $f(x)$ is defined as $f(x) = -7x^2$. What is $f(-2)$?

    F. -121

    G. -28

    H. 28

    J. 98

    K. 121

Take care to leave the parentheses when you plug in the value -2.

$-7(-2)^2$

According to the order of operations, exponents are resolved before multiplication.

$(-2)^2 = 4$

$-7 \cdot 4 = -28$

If you multiply before you resolve the exponent or if you drop a negative sign here or there, you can easily miss the question.

» PLUG AND CHUG

Sometimes the best way to approach a tricky algebra question is to plug in numbers.

Look at the answer choices and the question to think of the best numbers to plug in.

Once you choose a number, try it to see if it works with the question and answers. If your numbers come from the answer choices, start in the middle and move to higher or lower numbers if necessary.

If more than one choice works for one of your numbers, just pick a new number and try again.

Let's take a look at how this works on the ACT.

12. If $4^x = 52$, then which of the following must be true?

F. $1 < x < 2$

G. $2 < x < 3$

H. $3 < x < 4$

J. $4 < x < 5$

K. $x > 5$

The value 4^x is going to be equal to 52. The answer choices give ranges for the x value, so you should plug in the high and low to find the right answer. Start with the middle answer choice.

Start with choice H.

$4^3 = 64$ and $4^4 = 256$

Both of these are too large, so eliminate choice H. You can also eliminate choices J and K because they are even larger. Try choice G next.

$4^2 = 16$ and $4^3 = 64$

Since 52 is right between 16 and 64, you know this is the correct answer. There is no need to waste time trying choice F.

» HOW TO GUESS TWICE AS WELL

Here are a few guidelines that can help you to pick up many more points while guessing.

First of all, **these guidelines are not as good as actually solving the problem**. But if you don't have a clue, or if you feel like you've run into a brick wall, consider these:

- If you don't know the answer, **make your best guess before moving on**. You'll be much more accurate than if you blindly guess at the end of the test.

- **Never leave an answer blank.**

- Eliminate impossible answers. For example, if you know the answer must be negative, don't choose a positive number.

- If there are three possible answers left, *go with the middle one.* The test writers tend to "bracket" the answer choice.

NOTES

_____

_____

_____

_____

_____

_____

_____

_____

_____

_____

_____

_____

_____

_____

_____

_____

» ELIMINATE THE OUTLIERS

The writers of the ACT work really hard to come up with the **wrong answers** on all of the math questions.

They start with the correct answer and make some changes to it to make the wrong ones. Because of this, the correct answer is **almost always similar to the trickiest wrong answers.**

If you find yourself running out of time and need to guess, start by eliminating any answer choices that are **different from the others.** This won't always work, but it is your best bet to increase your chances of guessing.

Let's look at how guessing works on the ACT.

7. Which of the following mathematical expressions is equivalent to the verbal expression "A number, y, cubed is 42 more than the product of 13 and y"?

   A. $3y = 42 + 13y$

   B. $3y = 42y + 13y$

   C. $y^3 = 42 - 13y$

   D. $y^3 = 42 + y^{13}$

   E. $y^3 = 42 + 13y$

There are three outliers you should be able to notice in the answer choices: choice B with $42y$, choice C with $-13y$, and choice D with y^{13}. None of the other four choices contains those, so it is highly likely they are all wrong. Between choices A and E, if you are stuck and need to guess, choice E is the safer choice since it contains y^3, which shows up in more choices than $3y$.

Keep in mind, **this is a guessing technique.** You should **always** first try to solve questions before guessing, unless you are running out of time.

» DON'T SOLVE WORD PROBLEMS

Let's take a look at a commonly missed word problem and see how we can unlock its answer:

19. Mind Beats Audio is designing a box for its new line of professional headphones. The box is a rectangular prism that is 28 centimeters long, 19 centimeters wide, and has a volume of 6,384 cubic centimeters. What is the height, in centimeters, of the box?

A. 10

B. 12

C. 19

D. 48

E. 63

The key to this problem is identifying that we can take the words and convert them into an equation.

Always look for words that fit an equation or math rule you know. In this case, the volume formula applies.

Volume = length • width • height. We'll say that x = the height, which is the number we want to know.

$6,384 = 28 \cdot 19 \cdot x$

$6,384 = 532x$

$x = 12$

It's very difficult to solve a word problem. Math formulas and rules aren't about words: they're all about numbers and symbols.

Convert word problems into math problems, and then solve them. Convert what you know into the numbers in the equation (the constants and coefficients), and convert what you're trying to find out into symbols (variables).

In other words, express (say) the word problem as an equation.

Trying to solve a word problem before you set it up is like trying to run before you catch the ball.

Your first task with any problem is to set it up into something you can solve.

Only a one-two punch like this can knock out a word problem.

» DRAW IT OUT

It can be difficult to visualize word problems on the ACT Math test.

Many problems that involve a picture or shape don't actually show the picture in your test booklet.

That's what you call a lazy test writer! You have to do their job for them.

When the question discusses something that you can draw, immediately start drawing it out!

If the path to solving a question doesn't immediately pop out at you, drawing it out can make it more obvious.

Let's take a look at a problem that dramatically decreases in difficulty once you draw it out.

16. The base of a triangle is four times the base of a smaller triangle. The two triangles have the same height. The area of the smaller triangle is *A* square units. The area of the larger triangle is *kA* square units. Which of the following is the value of *k*?

F. ¼

G. ½

H. 1

J. 2

K. 4

First let's draw the two triangles and label the base and height of each.

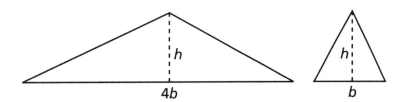

Since the area of a triangle is ½*bh*, we can plug in the values. Now that we have drawn it out, we don't have to keep referring to the text. We can use our illustration.

The area of the larger triangle is *kA* = ½4*bh*. The area of the smaller triangle is *A* = ½*bh*.

Since *A* = ½*bh*, we can substitute this in on the right side of the equation. We're left with this:

kA = 4*A*

Divide both sides by *A*.

k = 4

This problem is difficult to visualize, but if you draw it out it becomes much simpler to deal with.

» THE PROCESS OF ELIMINATION

- When you can't find the correct answer, **figuring out what is incorrect can be almost as good.**

- Knock out answer choices that are **unreasonable**, that **don't answer the question**, that are **negative when they need to be positive**, etc.

This process has many applications.

You can, for example, plug in answer choices and see if they cause both sides of the equation to equal out.

If they don't, then they're not correct.

You can also stumble into the correct answer doing this:

- **If you are going to guess and check, start from the middle and then work up or down** depending on whether your first guess was too high or low.

The key to eliminating answer choices is not being afraid to try them out and see if they work with the word problem.

If they don't, it's time to bid them farewell.

For example, let's look again at question 16.

16. The base of a triangle is four times the base of a smaller triangle. The two triangles have the same height. The area of the smaller triangle is A square units. The area of the larger triangle is kA square units. Which of the following is the value of k?

F. ¼

G. ½

H. 1

J. 2

K. 4

Since the area of the larger triangle is kA, and the area of the smaller triangle is A, we can eliminate answer choices F and G. kA has to be bigger than A.

Likewise, choice H doesn't work because that would mean that $kA = A$.

Now, if you have to guess, there are only two answers to choose from. This gives you a 50% chance of guessing correctly.

This page intentionally left blank.

21. In the triangle shown below, what is $\tan \theta$?

A. $\dfrac{a}{b}$

B. $\dfrac{a}{c}$

C. $\dfrac{b}{c}$

D. $\dfrac{b}{a}$

E. $\dfrac{c}{a}$

22. You observe your friend rolling on his skateboard at a constant rate along a straight, smooth street. As shown in the chart below, you record the distance as y feet of your friend moving from a particular reference point in one-second intervals from $t = 0$ seconds to $t = 5$ seconds.

t	0	1	2	3	4	5
y	3	12	21	30	39	48

Which of the following equations represents the data you record?

F. $3 + 9t$
G. $3 + 3t$
H. $9 + 3t$
J. $9 + 9t$
K. $12t$

23. Two lines, d and f, lie on the standard (x,y) coordinate plane. Line d has the equation $y = 2.34x + 567$. Line f has a slope that is 0.12 greater than the slope of line d. What is the slope of line f?

A. 2.35
B. 2.46
C. 3.54
D. 567.12
E. 568.2

24. In a soccer drill, 6 players stand evenly spaced around a circle. The player with the ball may pass it to any player who is not directly to his left or right. The player who last passed the ball cannot have it passed back to him immediately. A designated player begins the drill by passing the ball. What is the minimum number of passes (including the original pass) that must occur before the designated player has the ball again?

F. 2
G. 3
H. 4
J. 5
K. 6

25. The edges of a square are 4 inches long. One vertex of the square is located at $(3,1)$ on an (x,y) coordinate grid marked with 1-inch units. Which of the following points could also be a vertex of the square?

A. $(-1, -2)$
B. $(0, 3)$
C. $(3, -3)$
D. $(3, 6)$
E. $(7, 2)$

26. The expression $-7x^4(6x^3 - 4x^5)$ is equivalent to which of the following?

F. $-42x^7 + 28x^9$
G. $-x - 11x^2$
H. $-12x$
J. $42x^{12} - 28x^{20}$
K. $-42x + 28x^9$

27. $(2a + 3b - c) - (4a - b + 2c)$ is equivalent to which of the following?

A. $6a + 2b + c$
B. $-2a + 2b + 3c$
C. $-2a + 4b - 3c$
D. $4a - 2b + c$
E. $-4a - 2b + c$

28. The inequality $4(x + 3) < 5(x - 2)$ is equivalent to which of the following inequalities?

F. $x > -22$
G. $x > -2$
H. $x > 1$
J. $x > 2$
K. $x > 22$

GO ON TO THE NEXT PAGE.

29. $-5 \mid -2 + 7 \mid = ?$

   A. −45
   B. −25
   C. 0
   D. 25
   E. 45

30. In the right triangle $\triangle ABC$, $\overline{DE}$ is parallel to $\overline{AB}$, and $\overline{DE}$ is perpendicular to $\overline{BC}$. The length of $\overline{AC}$ is 26 inches, the length of $\overline{DC}$ is 12 inches, and the length of $\overline{DE}$ is 5 inches. What is the length of $\overline{AB}$?

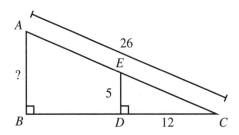

   F. 5
   G. 6
   H. 10
   J. 15
   K. 18

END OF TEST
STOP! DO NOT GO ON TO THE NEXT PAGE
UNTIL TOLD TO DO SO.

» DISTRIBUTIVE PROPERTY: HOW PARENTHESES SHARE

- **Use the distributive property when you need to get rid of parentheses.**

A clue that you need to use this procedure is that the ACT will ask you to simplify an expression that has parentheses, and none of the answer choices will have parentheses.

With the distributive property, you actually distribute (share) the coefficient of the group of terms in parentheses among each of the individual elements (members) of the group.

Share the wealth!

For example:

$$3(2x + 5) = (3)(2x) + (3)(5)$$

$$(3)(2x) + (3)(5) = 6x + 15$$

Be cautious about keeping the negative signs straight.

$$-4(x - 4) = (-4)(x) - (-4)(4)$$

$$(-4)(x) - (-4)(4) = -4x - (-16)$$

$$-4x - (-16) = -4x + 16$$

Try to **keep the distributed terms in parentheses** until you're actually doing your operations so that you can't make a mistake.

Let's take a look at this tricky question:

27. $(2a + 3b - c) - (4a - b + 2c)$ is equivalent to which of the following?

    A. $6a + 2b + c$

    B. $-2a + 2b + 3c$

    C. $-2a + 4b - 3c$

    D. $4a - 2b + c$

    E. $-4a - 2b + c$

The minus sign applies to everything that is in the second set of parentheses. *Remember that subtracting is the same as adding the negative version of the same number.*

$$8 - 4 = 8 + (-4)$$

For that reason, you can do the same trick to simplify your distributive property procedure.

Flip the minus into a plus sign.

$(2a + 3b - c) + (-1)(4a - b + 2c)$

Now distribute the −1.

$2a + 3b - c + (-1)(4a) - (-1)(b) + (-1)(2c)$

$2a + 3b - c + (-4a) - (-1b) + (-2c)$

Combine like terms.

$-2a + 4b - 3c$

By taking one step at a time, you can avoid the mistakes that cause inaccuracies on the ACT.

NOTES

_____

_____

_____

_____

_____

_____

_____

_____

_____

_____

_____

_____

_____

_____

_____

» TWO TRIANGLES OF A FEATHER

- Similar triangles have congruent (identical) angles.

- Their side lengths are proportional.

In other words, if one side of triangle *A* has a length of 3, and triangle *B* is similar with a matching side length of 6, then ALL of the side lengths of triangle *B* are twice the length of triangle *A*'s matching sides.

- **You can figure out the lengths of one triangle by comparing them to the lengths of another similar triangle.**

Be on the lookout for triangles that have identical angles, even if the ACT doesn't tell you that this is the case.

- Embedding triangles is a common way the test hides similar triangles.

Let's take a look at this practice question.

30. In the right triangle $\triangle ABC$, $\overline{DE}$ is parallel to $\overline{AB}$, and $\overline{DE}$ is perpendicular to $\overline{BC}$. The length of $\overline{AC}$ is 26 inches, the length of $\overline{DC}$ is 12 inches, and the length of $\overline{DE}$ is 5 inches. What is the length of $\overline{AB}$?

F.   5

G.   6

H. 10

J.   15

K. 18

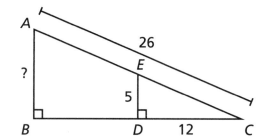

The first step to solving this problem is recognizing that $\triangle ABC$ is similar to $\triangle EDC$. That means that if you can figure out the ratio of the lengths between the two triangles, you can figure out the length of $\overline{AB}$.

Work backward from this idea. If we could figure out the length of $\overline{EC}$, then we would know the ratio. Use the Pythagorean theorem to find the length of $\overline{EC}$:

$5^2 + 12^2 = c^2$

$c^2 = 169$

$c = 13$

The bigger triangle has twice the length of the smaller triangle. Therefore, the length of $\overline{AB} = 5 \cdot 2 = 10$.

» EQUATIONS WITHOUT EQUALS

When you have to simplify inequalities, remember that **you can treat them like equations, with two special rules:**

- **If you multiply or divide both sides by a negative number, you have to flip the inequality sign.**

That's because, for example, $-5 < -4$, but $5 > 4$.

- Also, unlike with equations, **you can't flip the sides of an inequality without also flipping the sign.**

That's because $5 > 4$ but $4 < 5$.

Keep these two rules in mind, and you can solve inequalities on the ACT just as easily as you can solve equations.

For example:

28. The inequality $4(x + 3) < 5(x - 2)$ is equivalent to which of the following inequalities?

    F. $x > -22$

    G. $x > -2$

    H. $x > 1$

    J. $x > 2$

    K. $x > 22$

First we must simplify this using the distributive property.

$(4)(x) + (4)(3) < (5)(x) - (5)(2)$

$4x + 12 < 5x - 10$

Subtract $4x$ from both sides and add 10.

$22 < x$

Flip the inequality to make it match one of the answer choices.

$x > 22$

» MAKE A MAP

Some ACT problems refer to a shape or figure that appears on the coordinate plane.

They will typically refer to *specific coordinates.*

The questions might also talk about *moving up or down a certain number of units.*

Don't try to visualize all of this! (Unless you have coordinate planes tattooed on the back of your eyelids.) Draw it out.

Sketch a little coordinate plane and count out dots along the *x*- and *y*-axes in order to draw the shapes being talked about.

In other words, *make your own little map.* You don't have graph paper, but you don't need to be that precise.

This is a special version of drawing it out. **It's always worth the small amount of time it takes to sketch your graph** because doing so makes it more certain you'll put this question in the bag.

Let's take a look at this example question from the mini-test:

25. The edges of a square are 4 inches long. One vertex of the square is located at (3,1) on an (*x,y*) coordinate grid marked with 1-inch units. Which of the following points could also be a vertex of the square?

A. (−1,−2)

B. (0,3)

C. (3,−3)

D. (3,6)

E. (7,2)

Once you draw this out, it becomes obvious that (3,−3) could work. A square has lengths of equal sides, so the new point needs to be 4 units away from the point we start with.

Remember that *a vertex is just a corner of a shape.* It's a point where two line segments meet.

» SIMPLE, COSTLY MISTAKES

Errors in calculation and dropping negative signs can cost you a point or more on the ACT Math test.

Take these simple steps to make sure these mistakes don't happen to you.

1. **Use the calculator to work operations that go beyond simple arithmetic.**

2. **Do only one calculator operation at a time, and write out the result of each calculation as you go.**

3. **If the problem involves a negative sign, triple check to make sure you haven't accidentally dropped one or let it slip.**

4. **If the problem involves an inequality, double check that you have the sign pointing the right way.**

5. **Stay on high alert for technicalities. For example, $a \geq$ sign is graphed with a closed dot, but $a >$ sign is graphed with an open dot. Keep in mind the little mistakes you've made here and there in your math classes, and watch out for them in your ACT math work.**

6. **Once you finish your math test, work back through it, verifying your answers. *Don't just repeat the steps you already took.* Try different answer choices and make sure they don't work. Challenge yourself to find something wrong with your answer.**

NOTES

_____

_____

_____

_____

_____

_____

_____

_____

_____

_____

31. On the standard (x,y) coordinate plane below, which of the following quadrants contain all of the points found on the line $-3x + 5y = 15$?

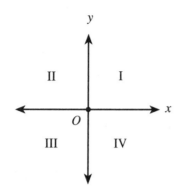

A. I and III
B. I, II, and III
C. I, II, and IV
D. I, III, and IV
E. II, III, and IV

32. In the rhombus $ABCD$ below, $\overline{AB} = \overline{BC} = \overline{CD} = \overline{AD}$. F is the midpoint of $\overline{AB}$, G is the midpoint of $\overline{BC}$, H is the midpoint of $\overline{CD}$, and E is the midpoint of $\overline{AD}$. $\overline{FH}$, $\overline{GE}$, $\overline{BD}$, and $\overline{AC}$ intersect at the same point, O. In the figure shown below, what is the ratio of the area of the non-shaded region to the area of the shaded region?

F. 1:2
G. 1:3
H. 1:4
J. 1:6
K. 1:8

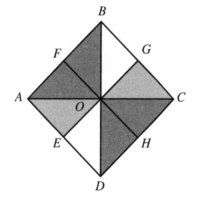

33. A bag contains 8 gold coins, 28 silver coins, and 22 copper coins. How many gold coins must be added to the 58 coins already in the bag in order for a 2/7 probability of randomly drawing a gold?

A. 8
B. 10
C. 12
D. 16
E. 22

34. A pool consisting of a square and two semicircles has dimensions shown below. What is the outside perimeter, in meters, of the pool?

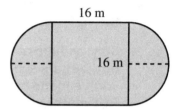

F. $16 + 8\pi$
G. $16 + 16\pi$
H. $32 + 16\pi$
J. $32 + 32\pi$
K. $64 + 32\pi$

35. The coordinates of the endpoints of line segment f, in the standard (x,y) coordinate plane, are (4,3) and (–8,9). What is the x coordinate of the midpoint of line segment f?

A. –4
B. –2
C. 0
D. 3
E. 4

36. The equation of a certain circle in the standard (x,y) coordinate plane is $(x - 1)^2 + (y + 2)^2 = 25$. Find the radius and center of the circle.

F. $r = 25$; (1,2)
G. $r = 25$; (1,–2)
H. $r = 5$; (–1,2)
J. $r = 5$; (1,–2)
K. $r = 5$; (1,2)

GO ON TO THE NEXT PAGE.

37. The graph of the equation $y = -3x^2 + 17$ passes through the point $(1, 7a)$ in the standard (x,y) coordinate plane. What is the value of a?

A. 1
B. 2
C. 3
D. 4
E. 7

38. What is the surface area, in square centimeters, of a 7 centimeter cube?

F. 7
G. 49
H. 196
J. 294
K. 343

39. Megan, Emily, and Melanie share a container of ice cream. Megan eats $\frac{1}{8}$ of the container, Emily eats $\frac{1}{4}$ of the container, and Melanie eats the rest. What is the ratio of Megan's share to Emily's share to Melanie's share?

A. 1:2:5
B. 1:1:5
C. 2:2:5
D. 5:1:1
E. 5:2:1

40. For $\triangle ABC$, shown below, which of the following is an expression for y in terms of x?

F. $\sqrt{x^2 - 49}$

G. $\sqrt{x^2 + 49}$

H. $\sqrt{x^2 - 7}$

J. $\sqrt{x^2 + 7}$

K. $\sqrt{x - 7}$

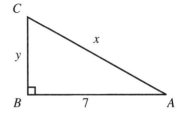

END OF TEST
STOP! DO NOT GO ON TO THE NEXT PAGE
UNTIL TOLD TO DO SO.

» Y IN TERMS OF X

Let's take a look at a problem that uses the expression **y *in terms of* x**.

40. For $\triangle ABC$, shown below, which of the following is an expression for y in terms of x?

F. $\sqrt{x^2 - 49}$

G. $\sqrt{x^2 + 49}$

H. $\sqrt{x^2 - 7}$

J. $\sqrt{x^2 + 7}$

K. $\sqrt{x - 7}$

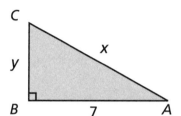

This expression simply means "show me what y is equal to using only x's."

It's also telling you that your answer will probably have an x in it.

- *In terms of* in this sense means "using" or "expressed with."

We don't have to figure out a number value for x in this problem. We only need to get y by itself on one side of the equation.

Since the Pythagorean theorem tells us that $a^2 + b^2 = c^2$,

$y^2 = x^2 - 7^2$

$y^2 = x^2 - 49$

$y = \sqrt{x^2 - 49}$

By the way, another tricky word to look out for is "real."

"Real" refers to the set of all numbers except imaginary numbers. "Imaginary numbers" are those that include the square root of –1.

If the ACT says "real," you can *usually* just scratch through the word.

The test writer is just referring to any number.

» HIDDEN ALGEBRA

Just because a problem involves the coordinate plane or a slope formula doesn't mean that it isn't basically an algebra problem.

- **Lines graphed on the coordinate plane are based on equations.**

- The line on the plane shows all of the possible solutions for that particular equation.

- When you know the value of an x-coordinate that lies on the line, you can plug it in as x in the equation and then solve for y.

The y value you obtain is paired with the x-coordinate for that point on the line.

Let's take a look at how we can plug in coordinates and then use algebra to solve the problem.

37. The graph of the equation $y = -3x^2 + 17$ passes through the point $(1, 7a)$ in the standard (x, y) coordinate plane. What is the value of a?

A. 1

B. 2

C. 3

D. 4

E. 7

For problems that look like this, with an equation with two variables as well as an (x, y) coordinate, simply plug in the x and y coordinate values.

If the path to the answer isn't apparent, walk through the open door.

In this case, we have an equation with an x and y value, and we have possible values for x and y, so let's plug them in.

$7a = -3(1)^2 + 17$

Use the correct order of operations. Resolve the exponent before multiplying.

$7a = -3 + 17$

$7a = 14$

Divide both sides by 7.

$a = 2$

Although this looked like a geometry problem, the bulk of the work was algebra!

» MAKE RATIOS SIMPLE

Try this trick next time you are having trouble deciphering a ratio problem like the one below:

39. Megan, Emily, and Melanie share a container of ice cream. Megan eats $\frac{1}{8}$ of the container, Emily eats $\frac{1}{4}$ of the container, and Melanie eats the rest. What is the ratio of Megan's share to Emily's share to Melanie's share?

A. 1:2:5

B. 1:1:5

C. 2:2:5

D. 5:1:1

E. 5:2:1

- **Instead of keeping everything as ratios, assume a length or number for one of the values described by the ratio.**

Let's say there are 8 ounces of ice cream in the container.

Then Megan gets 1 ounce, Emily gets 2 ounces, and Melanie eats 5 ounces. The ratio is 1:2:5.

It can be easy to get mixed up on ratios unless you assume a number to work with.

To use this technique, work out everything as it would be with that assumed value, making sure to keep all of the ratios true.

Then answer the question based on the information that you get from using this technique. You'll find that most ratio problems become much simpler to work with.

Try to use numbers that will be easy to multiply and divide with in order to move through the question as quickly as possible.

» OBJECTS IN MIRROR ARE EXACTLY AS THEY APPEAR

Every ACT Math test begins with this little disclaimer: "Illustrative figures are NOT necessarily drawn to scale."

- That being said, in almost all cases, **illustrative figures ARE drawn to scale**, and you can use this fact to answer correctly without having to know the geometry rules involved.

For example, if you are looking at a *narrow angle* on the test, don't select an answer that describes a *wide angle*.

You can also ballpark the dimensions of lines and angles straight from the illustration.

To enhance your ability to do this, grab a protractor and spend an hour learning how to eyeball the value of different angles. When you take the actual test, you can use your pencil as a ruler and the corner of your paper as a protractor.

Let's look at how we can apply this to the problem below:

32. In the rhombus *ABCD* below, $\overline{AB} = \overline{BC} = \overline{CD} = \overline{AD}$. *F* is the midpoint of $\overline{AB}$, *G* is the midpoint of $\overline{BC}$, *H* is the midpoint of $\overline{CD}$, and *E* is the midpoint of $\overline{AD}$. $\overline{FH}$, $\overline{GE}$, $\overline{BD}$, and $\overline{AC}$ intersect at the same point, *O*. In the figure shown below, what is the ratio of the area of the non-shaded region to the area of the shaded region?

F. 1:2

G. 1:3

H. 1:4

J. 1:6

K. 1:8

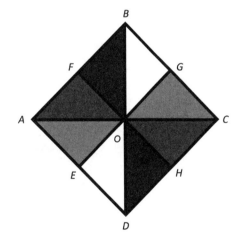

AB ∥ EG ∥ DC

BC ∥ FH ∥ AD

You can actually eyeball this shape and see that ¼ of the area is not shaded. For that reason, 1 part is not shaded for every 3 parts shaded, or a 1:3 ratio.

41. In the figure below, line $AD \parallel BE$, $\overline{AC}$ bisects $\angle DAB$, and $\overline{BC}$ bisects $\angle ABE$. If the measure of $\angle DAB$ is 76°, what is the measure of $\angle ACB$?

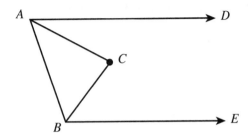

  A. 60°
  B. 70°
  C. 80°
  D. 90°
  E. 100°

42. The equations below are linear equations of a system where a, b, c, and d are positive integers.

$$ay + bx = c$$
$$ay + bx = d$$

Which of the following could possibly describe the graph of the above linear system in the standard (x,y) coordinate plane?

  I. 2 parallel lines
  II. 2 lines intersecting at a single point
  III. A single line

  F. I only
  G. II only
  H. I & II
  J. I & III
  K. II & III

43. For which value of b would the following system of equations have an infinite number of solutions?

$$y - 3x = 4$$
$$-2y + 6x = 2b$$

  A. −4
  B. −2
  C. 0
  D. 2
  E. 4

44. In the circle below, chords $\overline{AB}$ and $\overline{CD}$ intersect at the point O, which is the center of the circle. The measure of $\angle OCB$ is 25°. What is the degree measure of the minor arc $\overparen{DB}$?

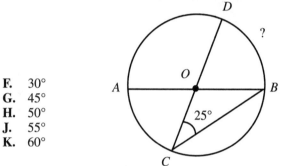

  F. 30°
  G. 45°
  H. 50°
  J. 55°
  K. 60°

45. According to the measurements given in the figure below, which of the following expressions gives the distance, in meters, from the cinema to the bookstore?

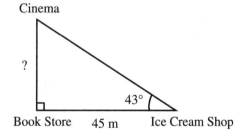

  A. $45 \cdot \tan 43°$

  B. $\dfrac{\tan 43°}{45}$

  C. $45 \cdot \cos 43°$

  D. $\dfrac{\cos 43°}{45}$

  E. $\dfrac{\sin 43°}{45}$

GO ON TO THE NEXT PAGE.

Use the following information to answer questions 46–48.

The figure below shows an emblem that is being designed for a company logo. It features a square inscribed within a diamond, which is inscribed in a circle, which is inscribed within a square. The edges of the outside square are 4 inches in length.

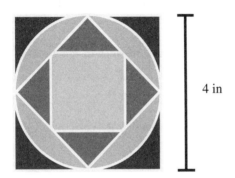

4 in

46. The emblem has how many lines of symmetry, discounting any text that might eventually be used in the logo?

F. 2
G. 3
H. 4
J. 6
K. 8

47. What is the area of the shaded region outside of the circle in the emblem, to the nearest 0.1 square inch?

A. 2.6
B. 3.4
C. 4.8
D. 5.2
E. 6.4

48. The company wants to create a sign from the image to be posted in front of its building. The length of each edge is to be 400% of its original size. What will be the area of the new sign, in square inches?

F. 64
G. 128
H. 256
J. 448
K. 512

49. You conduct a survey at your school of music types your classmates prefer. Your results are shown below in the circle graph. Based on the information already gathered, if you were to survey another student, what are the odds that this student would prefer pop music (pop music:not pop music)?

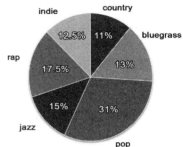

A. 69:31
B. 31:69
C. 3:1
D. 1:3
E. 1:1

50. Triangles $\triangle ABC$ and $\triangle EFG$ are shown below with side lengths x and y. The area of $\triangle ABC$ is 60 square meters. What is the area of $\triangle EFG$, in square meters?

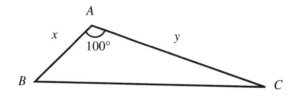

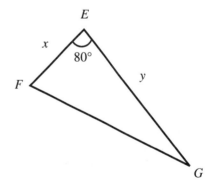

F. 40
G. 45
H. 58
J. 60
K. 75

GO ON TO THE NEXT PAGE.

Use the following information to answer questions 51–53.

In a factory, Noah can construct tablets in two sizes: large and mini. It takes 1 hour to construct a large tablet and 30 minutes to construct a tablet mini. The shaded triangular region shown below is the graph of a system of inequalities representing daily constraints Noah has in constructing the tablets. For making L large tablets and M tablet minis, the company makes $180L + 120M$ dollars in profit.

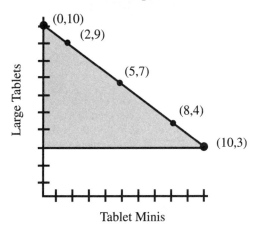

51. The daily constraint represented by the horizontal line segment containing the point (10,3) means that each day, Noah constructs a minimum of:

   A. 2 large tablets.
   B. 3 large tablets.
   C. 10 large tablets.
   D. 3 tablet minis.
   E. 10 tablet minis.

52. Today, Noah constructed 8 tablet minis and 4 large tablets. Assuming he spent all of his time constructing these tablets, how many hours did he work today?

   F. 6 hours, 30 minutes
   G. 7 hours
   H. 8 hours
   J. 8 hours, 30 minutes
   K. 9 hours

53. What profit does the company make when Noah constructs 10 large tablets, in dollars?

   A. 1,300
   B. 1,550
   C. 1,680
   D. 1,720
   E. 1,800

54. $\triangle LMN$ is shown in the figure below. The measure of $\angle N$ is 45°, $MN = 20$ cm, and $LN = 15$ cm. Which of the following is the measure, in centimeters, of $\overline{LM}$?

   (Note: For a triangle with sides of length a, b, and c opposite angles A, B, and C, respectively, the law of sines states that $\dfrac{\sin A}{a} = \dfrac{\sin B}{b} = \dfrac{\sin C}{c}$ and the law of cosines states $c^2 = a^2 + b^2 - 2ab \cdot \cos C$.)

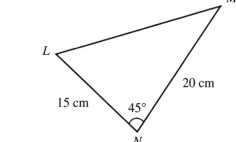

   F. $15 \cdot \sin 45°$
   G. $20 \cdot \sin 45°$
   H. $\sqrt{15^2 - 20^2}$
   J. $\sqrt{15^2 + 20^2}$
   K. $\sqrt{15^2 + 20^2 - 2(15)(20)\cos 45°}$

55. In the equation $x^2 + px + k = 0$, p and k are integers. The only possible value for x is 4. What is the value of p?

   A. −8
   B. −4
   C. −2
   D. 2
   E. 4

GO ON TO THE NEXT PAGE.

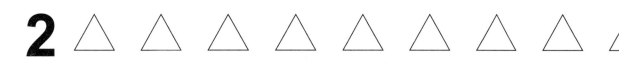

56. If a and b are real numbers such that $a > 2$ and $b < -2$, then which inequalitiy must be true?

F. $\dfrac{a}{b} > 2$

G. $2|a| > 2|b|$

H. $a^2 < b^2$

J. $a^2 - b < b^2 + a$

K. $\dfrac{a}{2} - 2 > \dfrac{b}{2} - 2$

57. The formula for finding the future value A of a principal value P with compound interest is $A = P(1 + \dfrac{r}{n})^{nt}$. Which of the following is an expression of the principal value P in terms of A, r, n, and t?

A. $Atn + Atr$

B. $\left(\dfrac{1}{A}\right)^{nt} + \left(\dfrac{An}{A}\right)^{nt}$

C. $Ant + \left(\dfrac{An}{r}\right)^{nt}$

D. $A\left(1 + \dfrac{r}{n}\right)^{nt}$

E. $\dfrac{A}{\left(1 + \dfrac{r}{n}\right)^{nt}}$

58. What is the sum of the first 5 terms of the arithmetic sequence in which the 7th term is 7 and the 11th term is 10?

F. 18.75
G. 19.25
H. 20.00
J. 20.50
K. 21.75

59. The solution set of which of the following equations is the set of real numbers that are 6 units from −2?

A. $|x + 2| = 6$
B. $|x - 2| = 6$
C. $|x + 6| = -2$
D. $|x + 6| = 2$
E. $|x - 6| = 2$

60. The determinant of a matrix $\begin{bmatrix} f & g \\ h & k \end{bmatrix}$ equals $fk - gh$. Which of the following is a value for x in the matrix $\begin{bmatrix} x & x \\ x & 6 \end{bmatrix}$ so that the matrix has a determinant of 8?

F. −2
G. −1
H. 0
J. 1
K. 2

END OF TEST
STOP! DO NOT GO ON TO THE NEXT PAGE
UNTIL TOLD TO DO SO.

» MATH FUNDAMENTALS

It bears mentioning here that **unless you're able to move quickly through math questions and perform most fundamental arithmetic quickly in your head, the ACT Math test will give you trouble.**

For that reason, *if you find that you are having trouble with the math test despite a lot of prep*, you may want to double back and work through some basic speed exercises in addition, subtraction, multiplication, division, solving for one variable, and basic geometry problems involving angles.

Check out the math area of FreeRice.com for some practice with basic math. Each time you answer correctly, 10 grains of rice are donated to someone who needs them!

Ask your teacher for more resources with basic math questions.

Khan Academy is a great online resource that can help you fill in any gaps in your understanding of basic math.

Try to answer the questions you're provided as quickly as you possibly can.

Once you speed up with your fundamentals, you can work on going faster with more complicated word problems.

The key to this is to work on questions you know how to do. Your objective is to move faster and to answer everything accurately.

NOTES

_____

_____

_____

_____

_____

_____

_____

_____

_____

» MATH WRAP-UP

The ACT Math test is one of the more rewarding sections to prepare for.

There are certain skills that the ACT will always test for, and if you master these, your score will rise.

There's no limit to the amount of improvement you can make on your ACT Math score, so don't let this chapter be the last step of your prep for the Math test.

Time is of the essence on the ACT Math test. Your score does not depend only on whether or not you know the information. Improving your speed and accuracy can have a big impact on your success.

For further study on the ACT Math test, check out these resources:

ACT Math Mini-Tests on page 210

Mastery for the ACT Math by MasteryPrep

SnapCourse for the ACT Math Online

Competition Math for Middle School by J. Batterson

The Art of Problem Solving: The Basics by Sandor Lehoczky & Richard Ruscyk

NOTES

_____

_____

_____

_____

_____

_____

_____

_____

_____

» ANSWER EXPLANATIONS FOR MATH PRACTICE TEST

1. **The correct answer is B.**

   Printer A runs for 10 minutes, and Printer B runs for 10 – 3 = 7 minutes.

   Printer A prints 10 • 30 pages = 300 pages.

   Printer B prints 7 • 40 pages = 280 pages.

   300 + 280 = 580 pages.

2. **The correct answer is J.**

   Use the FOIL method.

   First: $5x • 5x = 25x^2$

   Outer: $5x • -3y^2 = -15xy^2$

   Inner: $3y^2 • 5x = 15xy^2$

   Last: $3y^2 • -3y^2 = -9y^4$

   This gives $25x^2 - 15xy^2 + 15xy^2 - 9y^4$

   Combine like terms. $15xy^2 - 15xy^2$ cancels out.

   $25x^2 - 9y^4$

3. **The correct answer is D.**

   First use the distributive property.

   $7(x - 7) = 7x - 49$

   $7x - 49 = -15$

   Add 49 to both sides.

   $7x = -15 + 49$

   $7x = 34$

   Divide both sides by 7.

   $x = \dfrac{34}{7}$

4. **The correct answer is F.**

   Every time the number of adults goes up by 1, the dollar amount goes up by 45. 45 should be multiplied by *a*.

   Similarly, every time the number of children goes up by 1, the dollar amount increases by 25. 25 should be multiplied by *c*.

   The sum of these two expressions gives the total daily admissions: $45a + 25c$.

5. **The correct answer is E.**

   Natalie's regular pay rate is $9.50 per hour. Her overtime pay is $1\frac{1}{2} = \frac{3}{2} = 1.5$ times her normal pay.

   That means her overtime pay rate is $9.50 • 1.5 = $14.25.

   She works 40 hours at her normal pay rate and 3 hours at her overtime pay rate.

   Total pay = $9.50 • 40 + $14.25 • 3

   $380.00 + $42.75 = $422.75

6. **The correct answer is H.**

   First determine how many discounted tickets were purchased. If x is the number of tickets,

   $6x = 72$, $x = 12$ tickets.

   James would have spent $72.00 + $54.00 = $126.00.

   Divide this price by the number of tickets.

   $\frac{126}{12} = $10.50

7. **The correct answer is E.**

   Write out exactly what is said in the sentence.

   "A number, y, cubed" gives y^3.

   "Is" gives equals.

   "42 more than the product of 13 and y" gives $42 + 13y$.

   So, we have $y^3 = 42 + 13y$.

8. **The correct answer is J.**

   The perimeter formula is $P = 2l + 2w$.

   The area formula is $A = l • w$.

   Plug in the known values into these two equations.

   $24 = 2l + 2w$

   $35 = l • w$

   We can solve this as a system of equations using the substitution method.

   $w = \frac{35}{l}$

   Substitute this value of W into the perimeter equation.

   $24 = 2l + 2\frac{35}{l}$

Multiply both sides by l.

$24l = 2l^2 + 70$

$2l^2 - 24l + 70 = 0$

Divide both sides by 2.

$l^2 - 12l + 35 = 0$

Factoring gives

$(l - 7)(l - 5) = 0$

$l = 7 \mid l = 5$

If $l = 7$, then $w = 5$.

If $l = 5$, then $w = 7$.

The longer side is 7 meters.

An easier way to solve this is to guess and check. The possible side lengths that would give an area of 35 are as follows:

1 & 35

5 & 7

The first possibility (1 & 35) produces a perimeter of 72, so that doesn't work.

The second possibility (5 & 7) produces a perimeter of 24, which works.

9. **The correct answer is A.**

Plug in the values where the variables appear in the expression:

$[(7) + (4)][(7) + (-5) - (4)] = (11)(-2)$

$(11)(-2) = -22$

It is simpler and faster to plug in the values first before multiplying the variables. If the values of variables are known, always plug in the values first.

10. **The correct answer is J.**

First calculate Jason's average project grade.

Project average = $\dfrac{245 + 215 + 220 + 224}{4} = \dfrac{904}{4}$

$\dfrac{904}{4} = 226$

Let x be the score he needs on the last project.

$\dfrac{904 + x}{5} = 226$

Solve this for *x*.

$x = 5 \cdot 226 - 904$

$x = 1{,}130 - 904$

$x = 226$

11. The correct answer is B.

Let the smaller integer be *x* and the larger integer be (*x* + 1).

We know that $x + 4(x + 1) = 84$.

Solve for *x*.

$5x + 4 = 84$

$5x = 80$

$x = 16$

$x + 1 = 17$

The integers are 16 and 17.

You can also use the guess and check method. First try the middle option (C).

$17 + 4(18) = 17 + 72$

$17 + 72 = 89$

This is too big, so try a smaller set of numbers (B).

$16 + 4(17) = 16 + 68$

$16 + 68 = 84$. This works.

12. The correct answer is G.

The question clues you in to the fact that you need to pay attention to the answer choices. When you look them over, it becomes apparent that you don't need to have an exact answer: you just need to find out what numbers *x* is between.

The simplest way to solve this is to work out the value of 4 raised to the different possible powers.

$4^1 = 4$

$4^2 = 16$

$4^3 = 64$

52 is between 16 and 64, so this implies that *x* is between 2 and 3.

$2 < x < 3$

13. The correct answer is D.

The sum of the interior angles of a triangle is 180°.

$\angle A + \angle B = 66°$

So, $\angle C = 180° - 66°$

$\angle C = 114°$

14. The correct answer is G.

Plug in –2 where x appears in the function and simplify.

$f(-2) = -7(-2)^2$

Be careful about your order of operations. Resolve the exponent first.

$-7(-2)^2 = -7(4)$

Also, watch out for that negative sign. Don't lose it. It's a common reason why students miss this question.

$-7(4) = -28$

15. The correct answer is E.

Multiply the number of options together. Use your calculator.

$5 \cdot 2 \cdot 4 \cdot 3 = 120$ different sundaes.

16. The correct answer is K.

Sketch the problem, then use the area formula to set up an equation.

Let the base of the small triangle = b, which means the base of the larger triangle = $4b$.

The triangles have the same height = h.

Smaller triangle: $A = \frac{1}{2} \cdot b \cdot h$

Larger triangle: $kA = \frac{1}{2} \cdot 4b \cdot h$

Plug in $\frac{1}{2} \cdot b \cdot h$ for A.

$k(\frac{1}{2} \cdot b \cdot h) = \frac{1}{2} \cdot 4b \cdot h$

Divide both sides by $\frac{1}{2} \cdot b \cdot h$.

$k = 4$

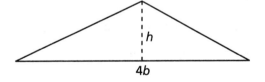

17. The correct answer is C.

Factor each number.

$30 = 3 \cdot 10$

$40 = 4 \cdot 10$

$70 = 7 \cdot 10$

The LCM is the smallest number that all of the given numbers go into. To find this, multiply all of the unique factors (so, in this question, you use 10 only once).

LCM: 3 • 4 • 7 • 10 = 840

18. The correct answer is J.

Since we want to know the value of y once 5 days have passed, plug in the value 5 for t.

$y = 21(3)^5$

Use the correct order of operations. Exponents before multiplication.

$21(3)^5 = 21 • 243$

$21 • 243 = 5,103$ bacteria.

19. The correct answer is B.

The volume formula is $V = l • w • h$.

$V = 6,384$ cm³, $l = 28$ cm, $w = 19$ cm, $h = ?$

Fill in the formula with the known values.

$6,384 = 28 • 19 • h$

$$\frac{6,384}{28 • 19} = h$$

$$\frac{6,384}{532} = h$$

Use your calculator.

$h = 12$ cm

20. The correct answer is K.

Sketch the problem.

Label point L first as it is the reference point for all other points given.

Clockwise means a circular motion where the top of the circle is moving right and the bottom of the circle is moving left.

Counterclockwise is the opposite: the top moves left while the bottom moves right. Try this with a ball if you find it difficult to remember.

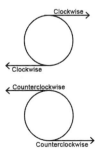
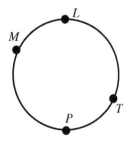

It does not matter where you place *L*.

M is 4 counterclockwise from *L*. *N* is 6 clockwise from *L*. *P* is both 9 clockwise and counterclockwise. In other words, *P* is directly across on the other side of the circle from point *L*.

Starting from *L* the points will read *N*, *P*, *M*.

21. The correct answer is A.

$$\tan \theta = \frac{\text{opposite}}{\text{adjacent}}$$

In other words, the tan function represents the fraction of the opposite side length over the adjacent side length.

a is the side opposite of the angle θ, and *b* is the side adjacent to the angle θ.

Therefore, $\tan \theta = \dfrac{a}{b}$

Keep in mind SOHCAHTOA if you have trouble remembering the definitions of the trig functions.

22. The correct answer is F.

Since *t* = 0 when *y* = 3, this is our initial position.

Eliminate the answer choices that don't equal 3 when *t* = 0. (That means you can knock out H, J, and K.)

Also, if you plug in the second value (*t* = 1), G doesn't work, since 3 + 3(1) = 6, not 12. Only the expression in F describes the results fully.

23. The correct answer is B.

The slope-intercept form is *y* = *mx* + *b*, where m is the slope and *b* is the *y*-intercept of the line.

In the given equation, *m* = 2.34.

For that reason, the slope of line *d* is 2.34.

If line *f* has a slope that is 0.12 larger than the slope of line *d*, that means the slope of line *f* is:

2.34 + 0.12 = 2.46

24. The correct answer is G.

Draw a circle with 6 evenly spaced points representing players. Let any player begin with the ball (it doesn't matter which one starts with it).

According to the rules, the player with the ball cannot pass to the players immediately to his left or right, and players cannot pass immediately back to the player who has just passed the ball.

The player who begins with the ball can pass to three different players.

At that point, the new player with the ball can't pass it right back. But once he or she passes it, the next person can pass it back to the original, *designated* player.

After trial and error, we see that the minimum number of passes before the original player receives the ball back is 3 passes.

The word *designated* means "chosen" or "selected."

25. The correct answer is C.

This is the only given point that is 4 units away from the given vertex.

The best way to answer this is to find a point that is 4 units away from (3,1).

Sketching it can help.

(3,–3) is 4 horizontal units to the left. All other answers are not 4 units away.

26. The correct answer is F.

Use the distributive property.

$-7x^4(6x^3 - 4x^5) = -42x^7 + 28x^9$

If you find yourself doubting your certainty of the exponent rules, remember that $x^4 = x \cdot x \cdot x \cdot x$

You can work this out using a long format in case you're unsure:

$-7xxxx(6xxx - 4xxxxx) = -42xxxxxxx + 28xxxxxxxxx$

Then add up your *x*'s.

$-42xxxxxxx + 28xxxxxxxxx = -42x^7 + 28x^9$

27. The correct answer is C.

First distribute the negative sign to the individual terms in the second grouping.

$(2a + 3b - c) - (4a - b + 2c) = (2a + 3b - c) - 4a + b - 2c$

We can simply drop the other set of parentheses because each term is effectively multiplied by 1 (the other grouping was actually multiplied by –1, which is what we had to distribute to each term).

Combine like terms.

$2a + 3b - c - 4a + b - 2c = -2a + 4b - 3c.$

This is an easy problem to confuse. Be careful with the negative signs and double check your work.

28. The correct answer is K.

Simplify using the distributive property.

$4x + 12 < 5x - 10$

Subtract 4x from both sides and add 10 to both sides.

$22 < x$

Flip the inequality to make it match the answer choice.

$x > 22$

Remember that, unlike with equations, when you flip the sides of an inequality, you also have to flip the sign.

29. The correct answer is B.

First resolve the operation inside of the absolute value.

$|-2 + 7| = 5$

$-5(5) = -25$

The absolute value operation gets resolved AFTER any operation inside of it. The -2 does not get turned into a positive 2.

First the -2 gets added to the 7. The absolute value of 5 is 5.

The absolute value of a negative number is that number multiplied by -1.

The absolute value of a positive number is simply that number.

30. The correct answer is H.

$\triangle ABC$ and $\triangle EDC$ are similar triangles. They have congruent angles.

If we can work out the length of EC, then we can compare it to AC and determine the ratio of the side lengths between the two triangles.

Since $\triangle EDC$ is a right triangle, we can use the Pythagorean theorem to find the length of EC.

$5^2 + 12^2 = c^2$

$169 = c^2$

Find the square root of both sides.

$c = 13$

Therefore, we can set up a proportion, letting the length of $AB = x$.

$$\frac{26}{13} = \frac{x}{5}$$

Multiply both sides by 5.

$$x = \frac{26 \cdot 5}{13} = 10$$

31. The correct answer is B.

To quickly interpret what a graph looks like, put its equation into slope-intercept form, $y = mx + b$.

$-3x + 5y = 15$

Add 3x to both sides.

$5y = 3x + 15$

Divide both sides by 5.

$y = \dfrac{3}{5} x + 3$

Now it's easy to draw the line. Sketch it directly on the picture. The y-intercept is 3, so draw that point. The slant of the line is gently upwards, since it's positive, but less than 1. We can see that the line passes through every quadrant except Quadrant IV. For that reason, B is the best answer.

32. The correct answer is G.

From the information given, it is clear that all of the 8 triangles formed in the figure are of equal area.

Two triangles are non-shaded while 6 are shaded.

This gives a ratio of 2:6 of non-shaded to shaded regions.

You can simplify 2:6 to 1:3.

33. The correct answer is C.

The easiest way to solve this is to guess and check. The number of gold coins added should be included in both the number of desired outcomes and the total number of possible outcomes in your probability fraction.

Always start doing guess and check with the middle answer.

There are 8 + 28 + 22 = 58 coins in the bag. Try 12 first since it's in the middle.

$\dfrac{8 + 12}{58 + 12} = \dfrac{20}{70}$

$\dfrac{20}{70} = \dfrac{2}{7}$

Therefore, 12 is the correct answer.

Another way to solve this problem is as follows:

The initial probability of drawing a gold coin is 8 / 58.

To find the value of x gold coins to add for a probability of 2 / 7, set up the following equation:

$\dfrac{8 + x}{58 + x} = \dfrac{2}{7}$

Next, cross multiply.

$7(8 + x) = 2(58 + x)$

Use the distributive property.

$56 + 7x = 116 + 2x$

Then, subtract $2x$ and 56 from both sides.

$5x = 60$

Finally, divide both sides by 5.

$x = 12$

34. The correct answer is H.

The perimeter of the pool is created by two sides of the square and two semi-circles.

Two semi-circles comprise one whole circle. So the perimeter of the pool is given by $16 + 16 + 2\pi r$.

The radius of the circle is 8. Plug this in as the value of r.

$32 + 2(8)\pi = 32 + 16\pi$

35. The correct answer is B.

The midpoint of a line segment is given by $(\frac{x_1 + x_2}{2} , \frac{y_1 + y_2}{2})$. The x coordinate of the these two points will then be $\frac{4 + (-8)}{2} = \frac{-4}{2} = -2$.

36. The correct answer is J.

The equation of a circle is $(x - h)^2 + (y - k)^2 = r^2$.

In this equation, the center of the circle is (h,k).

Therefore, this circle has a center $(1,-2)$. Radius is r.

$r^2 = 25$

$r = 5$

Be careful with the subtraction signs before h and k in the circle formula. They can be easy to mix up.

37. The correct answer is B.

A point on a line on the coordinate plane represents a solution to the equation that is provided. For that reason, you can always plug the values of the coordinate into the equation.

In this case, plug in 1 for the value of x and $7a$ for the value of y.

$7a = -3(1)^2 + 17$

$7a = -3 + 17$

$7a = 14$

Divide both sides by 7.

$a = 2$

38. The correct answer is J.

A cube is formed by six squares of equal area that are joined at their sides.

There are six squares of 7 • 7 square centimeter area.

So, the surface area of the cube is 7 • 7 • 6 = 294 square centimeters.

Don't mix this up with finding the volume of the cube. Surface area is the total area of all of the cube's faces. Volume is how much it holds inside. The volume of the cube is $7^3 = 343$, which would lead you to an incorrect answer choice.

39. The correct answer is A.

The simplest way to solve this problem is to assume an actual quantity of ice cream. Choose a number to multiply each fraction by so that they both become whole numbers.

Megan eats $\frac{1}{8}$ • 8 = 1.

Emily eats $\frac{1}{4}$ • 8 = 2.

Melanie eats the rest, which is 8 − 2 − 1 = 5.

Therefore, the ratio is 1:2:5.

Be sure to list Megan's share first! Choice E is the exact opposite of the correct answer and can be easily selected if you aren't careful.

40. The correct answer is F.

The phrase y *in terms of* x means "tell me what *y* means using *x*'s." In other words, you have to get *y* all by itself on one side of the equation.

Use the Pythagorean theorem.

$7^2 + y^2 = x^2$

$y^2 = x^2 - 49$

$y = \sqrt{x^2 - 49}$

41. The correct answer is D.

$\angle DAB = 76°$ gives that $\angle ABE = 180° - 76° = 104°$. (Extend lines *AB*, *AD*, and *BE* to make this more evident.)

$\overline{AC}$ bisects $\angle DAB$, so $\angle CAB = \frac{76°}{2} = 38°$. $\overline{BC}$ bisects $\angle ABE$, so $\angle ABC = \frac{104°}{2} = 52°$.

Interior angles of a triangle add up to 180°, so

$\angle ACB = 180° − 52° − 38° = 90°$.

42. The correct answer is J.

Note that both equations have a slope of b, meaning that these lines must be parallel to one another.

In the case that $c \neq d$, these are two parallel lines. However, in the case that $c = d$, these are the same line. They would have the same slope and the same y-intercept.

It is not possible for these lines to intersect at only one point. Since they have the same slope, they are parallel and, therefore, never intersect.

If you are having trouble visualizing these concepts, put the formulas into slope-intercept form.

Another tactic is to work to eliminate options I, II, and III. By plugging in a couple numbers for a, b, c, and d, you'll find that you can eliminate II, and that there is no other option.

43. The correct answer is A.

A system of two equations has an infinite number of solutions when both equations represent the same line.

In this case, you could imagine that the two lines intersect at every single point!

The goal in this problem, therefore, is to make the equations the same.

Notice that the left side of the top equation can be multiplied by −2 in order to make it match the left side of the bottom equation.

$(−2)(y − 3x) = (4)(−2)$

$−2y + 6x = −8$

Substitute −8 for $(−2y + 6x)$ in the second equation.

$−8 = 2b$

Solve for b.

$b = −4$

44. The correct answer is H.

Since $\triangle COB$ is an isosceles triangle (two equal sides), $\angle OCB = 25° = \angle OBC$.

Since the interior angles of a triangle add up to 180°, $\angle COB = 180° − 50° = 130°$.

$\angle COB + \angle DOB = 180°$

$\angle DOB = 180° − 130° = 50°$

The central angle is equal to the intercepted arc.

If you remember the rule about inscribed angles, then you can solve this much more quickly.

An inscribed angle is half of the intercepted arc. Therefore, since the inscribed $\angle DCB$ is 25°, then $\overarc{DB}$ has a measure of 50°.

45. The correct answer is A.

We are given the side adjacent to the known angle and want to discover the value of the side opposite the angle. So, we will use the tan function to find the distance between the cinema and the bookstore. Let x = the length we're trying to find out.

$$\tan 43° = \frac{x}{45}$$

$$x = 45 \cdot \tan 43°$$

46. The correct answer is H.

Draw a dot at the center of the emblem. Use your pencil to try different lines that result in a mirror image between one part of the figure and the other.

There are four lines of symmetry. One runs vertical through the midpoint. One runs horizontal. Two run from the corners of the outside square through the midpoint and across.

47. The correct answer is B.

Find the area of the square, then subtract the area of the circle inside of it in order to find the area of the shaded region.

The area of the square is $4 \cdot 4 = 16$.

The area of the circle, using the area formula $A = \pi r^2$, is $\pi 2^2 \approx 12.57$.

$16 - 12.57 \approx 3.43 \approx 3.4$

48. The correct answer is H.

The current edge length is 4 in.

Increasing this length to 400% its original length gives an edge length of 16 in.

That's because you can convert 400% to 4.00 then multiply that by the side length of 4 in order to find the new length.

The area of this new sign is then 16 inches $\cdot$ 16 inches = 256 square inches.

49. The correct answer is B.

Since 31% of the surveyed students preferred pop music, that means $100 - 31 = 69\%$ do not. For every 31 students who prefer pop music, 69 will not. The ratio is 31:69.

50. The correct answer is J.

The trigonometric area formula for a triangle is $A = \frac{1}{2}ab \cdot \sin C$, where a and b are adjacent sides and C is the included angle. Therefore, the area of $\triangle ABC$ is

$60 = \frac{1}{2}xy \cdot \sin 100°$

Because $\sin 100° = \sin 80°$, this means

$60 = \frac{1}{2}xy \cdot \sin 80°$

The area of $\triangle EFG = 60$ square meters.

51. The correct answer is B.

Since the shaded region never falls below the horizontal line $y = 3$, this means Noah always constructs at least three large tablets daily.

52. The correct answer is H.

It takes Noah 30 minutes or .5 hours to construct a tablet mini and 1 hour to construct a large tablet. So he worked $8(.5) + 4(1) = 4 + 4 = 8$ hours today.

53. The correct answer is E.

The company earns profit based on the equation $180L + 120M$. When Noah constructs 10 large tablets, he constructs 0 tablet minis. Solve by plugging these known values in to the expression.

$180(10) + 120(0) = 1,800 + 0 = \$1,800$

54. The correct answer is K.

The law of cosines is appropriate for the given information. Plug in the known values.

$c^2 = 15^2 + 20^2 - 2(15)(20) \cdot \cos 45°$

$c = \sqrt{15^2 + 20^2 - 2(15)(20)\cos 45°}$

Be careful to check what answer choices are available. You don't have to simplify your answer past this point.

55. The correct answer is A.

If the only possible value for x is 4, then that means $x^2 + px + k = (x - 4)(x - 4)$.

FOIL this out to get $x^2 - 8x + 16 = 0$.

$p = -8$

56. The correct answer is K.

Since a is always greater than b, $\frac{a}{2} - 2$ will always be greater than $\frac{b}{2} - 2$.

The other answers can be eliminated through trial and error.

57. The correct answer is E.

The words *in terms of* A, r, n *and* t mean that you need to get *P* by itself on one side of the equation. In other words, the question asks what is equal to *P*.

Divide both sides of the formula by $(1 + \frac{r}{n})^{nt}$.

$$P = \frac{A}{(1 + \frac{r}{n})^{nt}}$$

58. The correct answer is H.

The formula for an arithmetic sequence is $a_n = a_1 + (n - 1)d$, where a_1 is the first term and *d* is the common difference.

We can use the information provided to create a system of equations.

Plug in the values of the 7th term and the 11th term to create the two equations.

$7 = a_1 + 6d$

$10 = a_1 + 10d$

Subtract the first equation from the second to solve for *d*.

$3 = 4d$

$d = .75$

Plug this value for d back in to the second equation to find a_1.

$10 = a_1 + 10(.75)$

$a_1 = 10 - 7.5$

$a_1 = 2.5$

Now that we know the first term, 2.5, and we know the common difference, .75, we can work out the first 5 terms.

$2.5 + 3.25 + 4.0 + 4.75 + 5.5 = 20.00$

59. The correct answer is A.

First figure out the two numbers that are six units from –2.

–2 + 6 = 4

–2 – 6 = –8

Find the answer choice that is true for these two values by trial and error.

In $|x + 2| = 6$, both 4 and –8 work as values for x, so it is the correct answer.

60. The correct answer is K.

The determinant of the matrix $\begin{bmatrix} x & x \\ x & 6 \end{bmatrix}$ given by $6x - x^2$.

We need to find a value of x which causes the expression to equal 8, so let's set it up as an equation.

$-x^2 + 6x = 8$

Set it up for factoring.

$-x^2 + 6x - 8 = 0$

$x^2 - 6x + 8 = 0$

$(x - 2)(x - 4) = 0$

$x = 2 \mid x = 4$

Therefore, 2 and 4 are acceptable answers. However, only 2 is an available answer choice, so choice K is the correct answer.

NOTES

_____

_____

_____

_____

_____

_____

_____

_____

_____

This page intentionally left blank.

Reading

» INTRODUCTION TO THE ACT READING TEST

The ACT Reading test checks your ability to read.

It's a reading comprehension test above all, and no number of reading strategies can overcome poor reading skills.

If you have some time before your ACT test, I recommend that you *double down on your reading.*

Bookworms have a definite advantage on this section of the ACT.

- **If you aren't reading at a college level, you may find some segments of this test to be difficult.**

- That being said, **understanding the question types and following the pacing techniques contained in this Boot Camp can make a big difference in your score.**

NOTES

_____

_____

_____

_____

_____

_____

_____

_____

_____

_____

_____

_____

_____

» THE FOUR S'S

The key to the ACT Reading test is to learn how to **skim and scan** passages and to use **support and scope** for selecting answers.

- **Skimming** a passage requires you to read the passage very quickly, only looking for the most important information. The easiest way to do it is to read the first sentence of each paragraph and just look at the rest of the words without carefully reading them.

- **Scanning** a passage is the way you search the passage to find information you need to answer a question. The easiest way to do it is to move your finger over every word until you find what you need.

- **Support** always comes from the passage, and it is used to pick a correct answer. The easiest way to find it is to scan the passage before selecting any answers.

- **Scope** is the section of the passage that contains the correct answer. Even if a choice is supported, it is out of scope if it doesn't answer the question. The easiest way to find the correct scope is to stay in the same paragraph as the support you find during your scan.

NOTES

» GOOGLE YOUR WAY TO A HIGHER SCORE

- The most important question on the ACT Reading test is *where?*

The answer to every single ACT Reading question is contained in the content of the passages.

That means that you need to remember *where* things are.

You need to mentally index the location of information as you read so that you can "google" where it is instantly when you need to find it.

Think of indexing as your **skim** and googling as your **scan.**

Be your own search engine and watch your score increase.

Where is much more important than *who, what, when, why,* or *how.*

Skim through the passage before you read the questions, paying attention only to the **general idea of what is being said, who is saying it,** and **where everything is situated.**

Practice this during your mini-tests in this Boot Camp.

NOTES

_____

_____

_____

_____

_____

_____

_____

_____

_____

_____

_____

» NEVER RUN OUT OF TIME AGAIN

- Every single passage on the ACT Reading test has questions you can answer.

It's essential that you get through the entire test and prevent yourself from running out of time.

The way to accomplish this is to imagine that **each passage is a container with 8 minutes in it.**

Until you reach the end of the test, *don't steal time from one container to work on another.*

After 8 minutes, you *have* to move on to passage 2, and so on, until you're all the way through the test.

The practice tests in this part of the Boot Camp will help you learn more about how to achieve this pace.

NOTES

_____

_____

_____

_____

_____

_____

_____

_____

_____

_____

_____

_____

_____

READING TEST
35 Minutes — 40 Questions

DIRECTIONS: There are four passages in this portion of the test. Following each passage you will be given a variety of questions. Choose the best answer to each question, then fill in its corresponding bubble on your answer sheet. Refer to the passages as needed.

Passage I

PROSE FICTION: This passage is adapted from the novel *The Brothers Karamazov* by Fyodor Dostoevsky, originally published as a serial by *The Russian Messenger* in November 1880.

Fyodor Pavlovitch Karamazov was a landowner well known in our district in his own day, and still remembered among us owing to his gloomy and tragic death, which happened thirteen years ago, and which I shall describe
5 in its proper place. For the present I will only say that this "landowner"—for so we used to call him, although he hardly spent a day of his life on his own estate—was a strange type, a senseless type. But he was one of those senseless persons who are very well capable of looking
10 after their worldly affairs and nothing else.

Fyodor Pavlovitch, for instance, began with next to nothing; his estate was of the smallest; he ran to dine at other men's tables, and fastened on them as a toady, yet at his death it appeared that he had a hundred thousand roubles
15 in hard cash. At the same time, he was all his life one of the most senseless, fantastical fellows in the whole district. It was not stupidity—the majority of these fantastical fellows are shrewd and intelligent enough—but just senselessness, and a peculiar national form of it.

20 Fyodor Pavlovitch's first wife, Adelaida Ivanovna, belonged to a fairly rich and distinguished noble family. How it came to pass that an heiress, who was also a beauty, and moreover one of those vigorous intelligent girls, so common in this generation, but sometimes also to be found
25 in the last, could have married such a worthless, puny weakling, I won't attempt to explain.

Adelaida Ivanovna Miusov's action was, no doubt, an echo of other people's ideas, and was due to the irritation caused by lack of mental freedom. She wanted, perhaps,
30 to show her feminine independence, to override class distinctions and the despotism of her family. And a pliable imagination persuaded her, we must suppose, that Fyodor Pavlovitch, in spite of his parasitic position, was one of the bold and ironical spirits of that progressive epoch, though he
35 was, in fact, an ill-natured buffoon. What gave the marriage piquancy was that it was preceded by an elopement, and this greatly captivated Adelaida Ivanovna's fancy. Fyodor Pavlovitch's position at the time made him specially eager for any such enterprise. To attach himself to a good family

40 and obtain a dowry was an alluring prospect.

As for mutual love it did not exist apparently, either in the bride or in him, in spite of Adelaida Ivanovna's beauty. This was, perhaps, a unique case of the kind in the life of Fyodor Pavlovitch, who was always of a voluptuous
45 temper, and ready to run after any petticoat on the slightest encouragement. She seems to have been the only woman who made no particular appeal to his senses.

Immediately after the elopement Adelaida Ivanovna discerned in a flash that she had no feeling for her husband
50 but contempt. The marriage accordingly showed itself in its true colors with extraordinary rapidity. Although the family accepted the event pretty quickly and apportioned the runaway bride her dowry, the husband and wife began to lead a most disorderly life, and there were everlasting scenes
55 between them. The young wife showed incomparably more generosity and dignity than Fyodor Pavlovitch, who got hold of all her money up to twenty five thousand roubles as soon as she received it, so that those thousands were lost to her forever.

60 It is known for a fact that frequent fights took place between the husband and wife, but rumor had it that Fyodor Pavlovitch did not beat his wife but was beaten by her, for she was a hot-tempered, bold, dark-browed, impatient woman, possessed of remarkable physical strength. Finally,
65 she left the house and ran away from Fyodor Pavlovitch with a destitute divinity student.

Immediately Fyodor Pavlovitch abandoned himself to orgies of drunkenness. In the intervals he used to drive all over the province, complaining tearfully to each and all
70 of Adelaida Ivanovna's having left him, going into details too disgraceful for a husband to mention in regard to his own married life. What seemed to gratify him and flatter his self-love most was to play the ridiculous part of the injured husband, and to parade his woes with embellishments.

75 "One would think that you'd got a promotion, Fyodor Pavlovitch, you seem so pleased in spite of your sorrow," scoffers said to him. Many even added that he was glad of a new comic part in which to play the buffoon, and that it was simply to make it funnier that he pretended to be unaware
80 of his ludicrous position.

GO ON TO THE NEXT PAGE.

At last he succeeded in getting on the track of his runaway wife. The poor woman turned out to be in Petersburg, where she had gone with her divinity student, and where she had thrown herself into a life of complete
85 emancipation. Fyodor Pavlovitch at once began bustling about, making preparations to go to Petersburg. He would perhaps have really gone; but having determined to do so he felt at once entitled to fortify himself for the journey by another bout of reckless drinking.

And just at that time his wife's family received
90 the news of her death in Petersburg. She had died quite suddenly in a garret, according to one story, of typhus, or as another version had it, of starvation. Fyodor Pavlovitch was drunk when he heard of his wife's death, and the story is that he ran out into the street and began shouting with hands
95 to Heaven: "Lord, now lettest Thou Thy servant depart in peace," but others say he wept without restraint like a little child, so much so that people were sorry for him, in spite of the repulsion he inspired.

It is quite possible that both versions were true, that
100 he rejoiced at his release, and at the same time wept for her who released him. As a general rule, people, even the wicked, are much more naive and simple-hearted than we suppose. And we ourselves are, too.

1. The point of view from which the passage is narrated is best described as that of:

   A. a concerned friend.
   B. a family member.
   C. an amused observer.
   D. Fyodor's second wife.

2. The passage contains recurring references to all of the following qualities of Fyodor Pavlovitch EXCEPT his:

   F. cruelty.
   G. selfishness.
   H. drunkenness.
   J. buffoonery.

3. The first two paragraphs (lines 1-19) establish all of the following about Fyodor Pavlovitch Karamazov EXCEPT that he was:

   A. a landowner.
   B. a senseless type.
   C. rich at the time of his death.
   D. married multiple times.

4. It can reasonably be inferred from the passage that the narrator finds the story he is telling to be:

   F. an especially tragic tale.
   G. a rather humorous and droll account.
   H. a cautionary tale well worth hearing.
   J. an endearing bedtime parable.

5. Based on the narrator's account, all of the following events occurred before Adelaida's leaving for Petersburg EXCEPT which of the following?

   A. Fyodor "got hold of" twenty five thousand roubles from Adelaida.
   B. Adelaida received a dowry from her family.
   C. Fyodor dined at other men's tables.
   D. Fyodor ran into the street and began shouting.

6. According to the narrator, with whom did Adelaida Ivanovna run away to Petersburg?

   F. A bohemian bourgeois
   G. An aspiring artist
   H. A destitute divinity student
   J. An enchanting engineer

7. When the narrator describes Fyodor as "always of a voluptuous temper, and ready to run after any petticoat on the slightest encouragement" (lines 44-46), he most likely means that:

   A. Fyodor was quick to become violently angry.
   B. Fyodor was easily influenced by others.
   C. Fyodor had an eye for beautiful clothing.
   D. Fyodor often chased after other women.

8. Details in the passage most strongly suggest that the people meeting Fyodor Pavlovitch Karamazov found him:

   F. congenial and bewildering.
   G. abhorrent and preposterous.
   H. delicate and amiable.
   J. astringent and pensive.

9. The narrator indicates that Adelaida discovered that she felt nothing for Fyodor other than:

   A. contempt.
   B. curiosity.
   C. disbelief.
   D. adoration.

10. According to the passage, stories told that Adelaida Ivanovna perished either from starvation or:

   F. typhus.
   G. pneumonia.
   H. influenza.
   J. tuberculosis.

END OF TEST
STOP! DO NOT GO ON TO THE NEXT PAGE
UNTIL TOLD TO DO SO.

» DETAILS, DETAILS: ONE QUESTION TYPE, ONE-THIRD OF YOUR SCORE

- The **most common question type** is what we call **"finding details."**

The test asks you to find a specific detail in the passage, or, more commonly, three specific details.

This question is a good example of this type:

3. The first two paragraphs (lines 1-19) establish all of the following about Fyodor Pavlovitch Karamazov EXCEPT that he was:

A. a landowner.

B. a senseless type.

C. rich at the time of his death.

D. married multiple times.

The key to answering this question type is to **recognize it** then *immediately go scanning for the details*.

Think of it like a treasure hunt.

The first paragraph of the passage includes the fact that Pavlovitch is a landowner and a *senseless type*. The second paragraph describes how he was rich at the time of his death. There are no details in lines 1-19 about multiple marriages.

- **Don't waste time trying to answer this question type from memory.** If you do, you'll still need to look and verify it.

This question type can mean easy points if you don't allow the questions to eat up your time.

This is the lowest difficulty level of question type, but it can also be a time trap.

Questions 2 and 5 are also great examples of this question type.

In the mini-tests that follow, work to identify this question type. There will be a few in each passage. These can be "gimmies" if you practice quickly finding the answers.

» REASONABLY INFERRED, OR THE LEAST WORST ANSWER

- The clue to this question type is the phrase, **"it can reasonably be inferred that…"**

Sometimes it's said in another way, such as "it's most likely that…"

Here is a good example of this question type:

4. It can reasonably be inferred from the passage that the narrator finds the story he is telling to be:

    F. an especially tragic tale.

    G. a rather humorous and droll account.

    H. a cautionary tale well worth hearing.

    J. an endearing bedtime parable.

- **"Infer"** means to make a **conclusion by using reason and evidence** rather than from straightforward statements.

For these questions, you have to take what you've read and **make your best guess**.

Your answer is just that: *an educated guess.*

It's rare that you'll feel wonderful about your answer choice.

For example, in the question above, you can reason out that the narrator uses language such as *ridiculous*, *comic*, and *ironical*, indicating that he likely finds his story to be *humorous and droll* (curious or unusual). There is no indication made of the story being *cautionary* or *endearing*. Additionally, although the narrator does use the word *tragic*, he never indicates that he genuinely feels that his story is a *tragic tale*.

Of course, the correct answer is not spelled out clearly in this passage. You have to go with what seems to fit best.

Chances are, if this question were turned into an open-ended response question, your answer might look unlike any of the multiple choice answers.

To avoid wasting your time overthinking these types of questions, ask yourself, **"What is the best out of the worst answer choices?"**

Passage II

SOCIAL SCIENCE: This passage is adapted from the book *The American Revolution* by Sir George Otto Trevelyan, which was originally published by *Longmans, Green, and Co.* in 1921.

The leaders of thought in America, and those who in coming days were the leaders of war, had all been bred in one class or another of the same severe school.

Samuel Adams, who started and guided New England
5 in its resistance to the Stamp Act, was a Calvinist by conviction. The austere purity of his household recalled an English home in the Eastern Counties during the early half of the seventeenth century. He held the political creed of the fathers of the colony; and it was a faith as real and
10 sacred to him as it had been to them. His fortune was small. Even in that city of plain living, men blamed him because he did not take sufficient thought for the morrow; but he had a pride which knew no shame in poverty, and an integrity far superior to its temptations.

15 Alexander Hamilton, serving well and faithfully, but sorely against the grain, as a clerk in a merchant's office, had earned and saved the means of putting himself, late in the day, to college.

Thomas Jefferson, who inherited wealth, used it to
20 obtain the highest education which his native country could then provide; entered a profession; and worked at it after such a fashion that by thirty he was the leading lawyer of his colony, and that no less a colony than Virginia. The future warriors of the Revolution had a still harder apprenticeship.

25 Israel Putnam had fought the Indians and the French for a score of years, and in a score of battles; leading his men in the dress of a woodman, with firelock on shoulder and hatchet at side; a powder horn under his right arm, and a bag of bullets at his waist, and, (as the distinctive equipment
30 of an officer), a pocket compass to guide their marches through the forest. He had known what it was to have his comrades scalped before his eyes, and to stand gashed in the face with a tomahawk, and bound to the trunk of a tree, with a torture-fire crackling about him.

35 From adventures which, in the back settlements, were regarded merely as the harder side of a farmer's work, he would go home to build fences with no consciousness of heroism, and without any anticipation of the world-famous scenes for his part in which these experiences of the
40 wilderness were training him.

Nathanael Greene, the ablest of Washington's lieutenants—of those at any rate who remained true to their cause from first to last—was one of eight sons, born in a house of a single story. His father combined certain humble
45 trades with the care of a small farm, and, none the less or

the worse on account of his week-day avocations, was a preacher of the gospel. The son excelled in diligence and manly sports. None of his age could wrestle, or skate, or run better than he, or stand before him as a neat ploughman
50 and skillful mechanic.

Under such literary and scientific guidance as he could find among his neighbors, he learned geometry, and its application to the practical work of a new country. He read poetry and philosophy, as they are read by a man of many
55 and great thoughts, whose books are few but good. Above all, he made a special study of Plutarch and of Caesar— authors who, whether in a translation, or in the original Greek and Latin, never give out their innermost meaning except to brave hearts on the eve of grave events.

60 Meantime the military chief upon whom the main weight of responsibility was to rest had been disciplined for his career betimes. At an age when a youth of his rank in England would have been shirking a lecture in order to visit Newmarket, or settling the color of his first lace
65 coat, George Washington was surveying the valleys of the Alleghany Mountains. He slept in all weathers under the open sky; he swam his horses across rivers swollen with melted snow; and he learned, as sooner or later a soldier must, to guess what was on the other side of the hill, and to
70 judge how far the hill itself was distant.

At nineteen he was in charge of a district on the frontier; and at twenty-two he fought his first battle, with forty men against five hundred and thirty, and won a victory, on its own small scale, as complete as that of Quebec. The
75 leader of the French was killed, and all his party shot down or taken. It was an affair which, coming at one of the rare intervals when the world was at peace, made a noise as far off as Europe, and gained for the young officer in London circles a tribute of hearty praise, with its due accompaniment
80 of envy and misrepresentation.

Horace Walpole gravely records in his *Memoirs of George the Second* that Major Washington had concluded the letter announcing his success with the words, "I heard the bullets whistle, and, believe me, there is something
85 charming in the sound."

Such were the men who had been reluctantly drawn by their own sense of duty, and by the urgent appeals of friends and neighbors, into the front rank of a conflict which was none of their planning. Some of them were bred
90 in poverty, and all of them lived in tranquil and modest homes. They made small gains by their private occupations, and did much public service for very little or for nothing, and in many cases out of their own charges. They knew of pensions and sinecures only by distant hearsay; and ribands
95 or titles were so much outside their scope that they had not even to ask themselves what those distinctions were worth.

GO ON TO THE NEXT PAGE.

11. Which of the following assumptions would be most critical for a reader to accept in order to agree fully with the author's claims in the passage?

   A. The skills required to live in the wild can be very beneficial for war.

   B. The pen is a much more powerful weapon than the musket or the saber.

   C. Men with humbled beginnings can be capable of great things later in life.

   D. Not everyone in the colonies was interested in independence from the British.

12. In the context of the passage, the statement "he did not take sufficient thought for the morrow" (lines 11-12) most nearly suggests people thought that Samuel Adams:

   F. frequently lost track of time.

   G. often showed up late for social events.

   H. always stayed up too late.

   J. did not devote sufficient attention to financial matters.

13. It can most reasonably be inferred from the passage that regarding the fathers of the American Revolution, the author's tone is:

   A. nationalistic.

   B. academic.

   C. depressed.

   D. optimistic.

14. The main purpose of lines 31-34 is to:

   F. provide examples of experiences that prepared Israel Putnam for the Revolutionary War.

   G. explain what it was like to fight the Indians and the French.

   H. demonstrate the cruelty in the process of scalping.

   J. tell stories regarding Israel Putnam's extreme bravery.

15. The main function of the tenth paragraph (lines 71-80) is to:

   A. introduce the figure of Horace Walpole.

   B. provide examples of Washington's military achievement at a young age.

   C. explain that Washington had many memoirs written about him.

   D. demonstrate that Washington was very good with words.

16. All of the following are recurring themes in the narrative about the fathers of the Revolution, EXCEPT:

   F. they became experienced at early ages.

   G. they lived in modest homes.

   H. they were well studied in matters of battle and academics.

   J. they had constant legal trouble in the colonies.

17. The passage indicates that, as a group, the fathers of the American Revolution entered into the conflict:

   A. reluctantly.

   B. abruptly.

   C. brazenly.

   D. shamefully.

18. According to the passage, after inheriting wealth, Jefferson used it to dedicate himself to the practice of which of the following?

   F. Medicine

   G. Carpentry

   H. Law

   J. Smithing

19. The passage states that Nathanael Greene studied all of the following EXCEPT:

   A. poetry.

   B. geometry.

   C. philosophy.

   D. engineering.

20. According to the passage, when Washington fought his first battle, it:

   F. resulted in scorn from his soldiers.

   G. resulted in hearty praise from London.

   H. resonated throughout the colonies.

   J. remained the most important battle in history.

END OF TEST
STOP! DO NOT GO ON TO THE NEXT PAGE
UNTIL TOLD TO DO SO.

» FIND ALL OF THE WRONG ANSWERS

The ACT Reading questions and answer choices can be nearly as long as the passage they refer to.

This becomes a lot of text to keep straight in your head. It helps to eliminate answers that are wrong so that you have fewer answers to consider.

- When you read the question, if the answer does not immediately jump out at you, **get to work finding all of the wrong answers.**

Sometimes the correct answer does not seem exactly right, but *the wrong answers will obviously be wrong.*

You can save time by working hard to eliminate the bad answers first.

For example, let's take a look at question 11:

11. Which of the following assumptions would be most critical for a reader to accept in order to agree fully with the author's claims in the passage?

    A. The skills required to live in the wild can be very beneficial for war.

    B. The pen is a much more powerful weapon than the musket or the saber.

    C. Men with humbled beginnings can be capable of great things later in life.

    D. Not everyone in the colonies was interested in independence from the British.

In this question, we can eliminate choices B and D because, while they might possibly be true, they're not supported by the passage. Neither assumption contributes to the reader's agreeing with the author's claims.

Choice A is definitely supported by the passage, but it is the wrong **scope**, since the question is about the entire passage and choice A only fits one small part of the passage.

Eliminate answers that either contradict the passage or don't correctly fit with what is being asked. You will then be left with fewer choices to decide between.

» READ BETWEEN THE LINES

- The type of question that asks you to *read between the lines* is intended to penalize the test-taker who skips the passage and dives straight into the questions.

Let's examine one of the practice questions in order to see how this plays out on a real ACT test:

13. It can most reasonably be inferred from the passage that regarding the fathers of the American Revolution, the author's tone is:

    A. nationalistic.

    B. academic.

    C. depressed.

    D. optimistic.

Nowhere in this passage does it say, "Hi, I'm the narrator, and I'm writing with an academic tone."

However, we *can* read between the lines. We can figure out the *implied* concept by examining what has been *explicitly* said. We are looking for the meaning or theme *behind* what is said.

In order to answer this question type, you will need to have **skimmed** through the entire passage and gained a general grasp of the **main ideas of the passage** and **each paragraph**.

In question 13, we can eliminate several choices. An *optimistic* tone would be one that is hopeful and excited about the future. A *depressed* tone indicates that the narrator thinks there's not much hope for the future. There is nothing in the passage which indicates that the author is communicating in either of these tones.

A *nationalistic* tone would show the author expressing pride in his nation. Again, nothing in the passage supports this choice, so choice B is the best answer.

Remember that when you are reading between the lines, there have to be lines that you are reading through! Choices A, C, and D are wrong because there is nothing in the passage that would lead you to believe that those answers are correct.

If you hadn't read the passage all the way through, you might be tempted to choose something other than choice B because you wouldn't know enough about the content to be able to eliminate answers with certainty.

The key to answering these questions that have no exact evidence in the passage is to **eliminate the answers that are definitely incorrect**. Usually there will be only one left.

When reading between the lines, **make sure there is only one step of reasoning between what the passage says and what you conclude**.

Suppose the passage says, "He didn't see any cars for quite some time. He closed down his lemonade stand early."

If the ACT asked you why he closed down his lemonade stand, an appropriate answer might be, "There were fewer customers than he expected," but it would be too much to assume, "There was a hurricane coming."

Your answer has to be implied by the passage, even though it isn't directly stated the same way that the answer expresses the thought.

The correct answer in this type of question has a clear, substantial reason why it's correct. It's supported by something in the passage. Likewise, the test writers ensure that there is a clear reason why each other answer is incorrect.

NOTES

_____

_____

_____

_____

_____

_____

_____

_____

_____

_____

_____

_____

_____

_____

_____

_____

_____

» HOW TO STOP OVERTHINKING

I have tutored many high-performing overthinkers who could not help themselves; **they constantly erased the correct answer** and went with the **wrong one** after spending minutes deliberating.

Go with your gut.

If you have trouble doing this, you need to build up your "gut confidence."

There is a simple exercise to do this:

> When you're doing your practice tests in this Boot Camp, if you feel the urge to change an answer but don't have a completely clear and convincing reason to do so, leave it be. Mark it with an asterisk.

When you're checking your answers, see how your "gut" did.

You might be surprised how much better you do if you trust your instincts.

- You need both **confidence** and **speed** in order to boost your scores on the ACT.

If you're an overthinker, try the above exercise during the rest of the Reading practice tests.

If you want even more practice with this, do the following exercise after the Boot Camp:

> Get the *Real ACT Prep Guide, 3rd Edition*. Take your time working through the Reading practice tests. Read the explanations not only for why the correct answer is correct but also for the test writer's reasoning for why the other answers are wrong.

If you do this with enough ACT Reading practice tests, your speed and certainty can improve enormously.

» TOUGHER THAN CONTRADICTIONS

Eliminate two answer choices, and you have made the reading question twice as easy.

- The ACT test writers are obligated to have a clear reason why one answer is correct.

- Likewise, they have to justify why each other answer is wrong. To do this, they typically insert things in the false answer choices that make them incorrect.

The wrong answer choices will contradict the passage or **will not appear in the passage at all.**

People who are running out of time accidentally make choices that contradict the passage, and *people who overthink make choices that have no bearing on the passage at all.*

Don't make these mistakes.

- **Eliminate answers that contradict the passage or don't have anything to do with it.**

It's tough to eliminate answers that have nothing to do with the passage. You won't feel like you have a concrete reason for doing so. If you don't do this, however, you'll be prone to overthinking the questions.

For example:

17. The passage indicates that, as a group, the fathers of the American Revolution entered into the conflict:

A. reluctantly.

B. abruptly.

C. brazenly.

D. shamefully.

We can eliminate D right away because there is no support in the passage to indicate that the fathers of the American Revolution felt shame about entering the conflict.

You can also eliminate choice C because while the passage might support that the fathers of the American Revolution were very bold, or brazen, this choice would not fit the **scope** of how they *entered into the conflict*, which was specifically described as *reluctantly*, making choice A correct.

This page intentionally left blank.

Passage III

HUMANITIES: This passage is adapted from *A Biography of Ralph Waldo Emerson: Set Forth as His Life Essay* by Denten Jaques Snider, originally published by the William Harvey Miner Company in 1921.

Emerson's total round of years does not quite run up to four score (1803-1882). Some way or other we must be led to see and to express the man's ultimate process as revealed in his character and stamped upon the whole of it and the
5 parts. A very intricate piece of humanity is our Emerson, labyrinthine, and somewhat gnarled in spots; but when seen and felt in the entirety of his existence, he integrates all its recalcitrant fragments, and attunes to one key-note its varied discords. His wholeness makes him whole in all his
10 seeming defections and his differences.

The life of the one person, especially if he be representative, is to be shown bearing the impress of supreme personality. To use an Emersonian conception, man's biography is an efflux of God's biography; the
15 finite Self, in its most intimate unitary act as well as in its diversified individual career must be seen reflecting the image of the universal Self. The events, doctrines, deeds of a man's life are a chaos till the biographer voicing the Supreme Orderer turns them into a cosmos.

20 Accordingly, the first task of the life-writer is to catch the primordial stages of this highest activity, which thereby becomes creative of his theme, and clothes itself in the special details of a human career. That is, we seek at the start to mark the great sweeps, the pivotal turns, the grand
25 crises of a life, which we shall call Periods. In other words, our first attempt is to periodize Emerson.

Let it be emphasized, then, that the most deeply significant node of Emerson's career hovers about the years 1834 to 1835 when he was passing through his thirty-
30 second year. After a good deal of drifting, both inner and outer, he finally established his home at Concord, home spiritual as well as domestic. He had won his fundamental conception, he had thought out his world-view, and was ready, eager to set it down in writing and to promulgate it to
35 the time despite all neglect and calumny. He was assured of his economic independence. He had both the leisure and the solitude to yield himself freely to the immediate impress of nature and deity, and to report the same as the true content of his life's work. In his own house at Concord, where he
40 settled, he had taken a lofty position, from which he could swoop down upon the outlying earth, and especially upon adjacent unreceptive Boston, capital of Philistia. Then he would return to his isolated perch for fresh meditation and writing. His abode becomes for him a Castle of Defiance,
45 also a Fortress of Liberty, quite impregnable by any sort of hostile gunnery or hunger.

Thus we set down the chief landmark in Emerson's biography, the transition of the young man into his middle life, into the time of his originality and main achievement—
50 his Second Period, as we shall name it, embracing quite three decades of his activity. Antecedent to his landmark and leading up to it rise Emerson's years of education at home and at college, his training to his transmitted vocation till his falling out with it and flight abroad. In general, this
55 stage stresses his appropriation of the traditional Past, against which, however, there runs in him an ever-increasing protest all the way up to downright revolt. At the same time through this negative schooling he is slowly evolving into his positive world-view or ultimate Idea, which he is to
60 proclaim to the ages from his perch of lofty independence on his Castle of Defiance.

There remains the final or Third Period of Emerson's life which he himself has indicated decisively in his poem named "Terminus." Under this title the God of Metes and
65 Bounds appears to him, commanding, "No more! No farther shoot thy ambitious branches and root." This was read to his son in 1866; already the poet had felt he had reached the last great turn of his career and cried out:

It is time to be old,
70 To take in sail.
Economize the failing river,
Mature the unfilled fruit.

In such words Emerson takes a survey of his time of life and declares what in general he is henceforth to perform
75 during his remaining days. He states the character and content of his Third Period, or that of his old-age, as distinct from his middle or Second Period. He is to go back and gather up what of his harvest still lies scattered. The time of creative power is past: "Fancy departs, no more invent.
80 Let there now be a return upon my former self, an era of collection and recollection, such as befits the graying hair of the sage."

Thus we glimpse the complete round of Emerson's youth, manhood, and age, the compartments of his life-cycle,
85 with their corresponding pivotal activities. Remember that it is the man himself looking backward and feeling deeply the turning nodes of his spirit, who thus draws his own life-lines and marks his Periods. Herein we may well hear him giving a hint for his future biography. Moreover these three
90 stages are to be seen finally as one process of Emerson's soul imprinted on his total achievement. Thus we may take up his last meaning into our own existence, which in its special way is passing through the same spiritual stages— we too are to have our measured and fulfilled allotment of days and their works.

GO ON TO THE NEXT PAGE.

21. The passage is best described as being told from the point of view of a biographer who finds Emerson to be:

    A. tedious.
    B. frustrating.
    C. admirable.
    D. confusing.

22. Based on the passage, to which of the following did Emerson choose to dedicate his life's work?

    F. The self and the soul
    G. Morality and ethics
    H. Poetry and prose
    J. Nature and deity

23. The main purpose of the third paragraph (lines 20-26) is to:

    A. define the first task of the biographer as laying out the subject's life.
    B. demonstrate an initial overview of Emerson's life.
    C. divide Emerson's poetry into thematic genres.
    D. discuss the main images in Emerson's poetry.

24. The passage indicates that, through his falling out with his vocation, increasing revolt, and negative schooling, Emerson:

    F. became an extremely reclusive figure.
    G. began to develop his ultimate Idea.
    H. fled society and disappointed his peers.
    J. was finally able to survey his life.

25. The author mentions Emerson's poem "Terminus" primarily to suggest:

    A. that Emerson had become rather depressed in his old age.
    B. that Emerson would likely be writing poetry from his deathbed.
    C. the way in which Emerson had become a capable poet.
    D. the nature of the transition from the Second to the Third Period.

26. In the first paragraph (line 5), when the author describes Emerson as "labyrinthine," he most nearly means which of the following?

    F. Information regarding Emerson is difficult to find.
    G. Emerson could sometimes be confusing or contradictory.
    H. Emerson never stayed in one place for long.
    J. Emerson's favorite hobby was wandering aimlessly through the forest.

27. Viewed in the context of the passage, the statement in lines 59-61 is most likely intended to suggest that:

    A. Emerson could be found shouting frequently in his home.
    B. Emerson never moved from his home after establishing it.
    C. Emerson was a gravely serious man that needed to be heard.
    D. Emerson began writing and publishing his newly developed ideas.

28. The author refers to Emerson and "the turning nodes of his spirit" in lines 86-87 as part of his description of:

    F. Emerson's examination of his own life.
    G. the battle of contradictions in Emerson's personality.
    H. the way in which Emerson chose to write his poetry.
    J. an example of the metaphors that Emerson utilized.

29. In the context of the passage, lines 69–72 provide metaphors which best describe:

    A. an aging man assessing his life.
    B. decaying fruit in a garden.
    C. a young boy's pullulating sense of wonder.
    D. a riverbed drying in the sun.

30. Which of the following is NOT used by the author to describe Emerson's home in Concord?

    F. His isolated perch
    G. A Castle of Defiance
    H. His Supreme Cosmos
    J. A Fortress of Liberty

END OF TEST
STOP! DO NOT GO ON TO THE NEXT PAGE
UNTIL TOLD TO DO SO.

» FINDING MEANING

The ACT Reading test checks your understanding of the **actual meaning of a paragraph or passage**.

- A way to simplify your work on this question type is to ask yourself, **"What is the author really trying to say here?"**

- Sometimes **vocabulary** that you are unfamiliar with can block you from having a full understanding of the paragraph in question.

- More frequently, **tough vocabulary in the questions and answer choices can throw you off.**

The key to wading through this is to refuse to get confused!

Work through your standard process of eliminating answers, keeping in mind that *it will be difficult to eliminate an answer choice with unfamiliar vocabulary*, **but it doesn't mean that an answer choice with difficult vocabulary is correct.**

If you have two choices left, and one is perfectly legitimate with nothing wrong in it, while the other has a strange word in it, go with the one that you understand and seems to work.

Don't fall into the danger of choosing a wrong answer just because it has an intimidating word.

For example, let's take a look at question 29:

> **29.** In the context of the passage, lines 69–72 provide metaphors which best describe:
>
> A. an aging man assessing his life.
>
> B. decaying fruit in a garden.
>
> C. a young boy's pullulating sense of wonder.
>
> D. a riverbed drying in the sun.

The best choice is A. In order to answer this correctly, you have to interpret the meaning of the lines. Ask yourself, "What is the author really trying to say here?"

Since a metaphor is a phrase or word that stands as a symbol for something, you should eliminate B and D (which are saying that the poem is talking literally about fruit and rivers instead of being a metaphor). The phrase *It is time to be old* contradicts C. However, the word *pullulating*, which means "lively and full," might throw you off. Don't choose it just because it's a tough word!

In these lines, the author is trying to communicate about being an aging man looking back over his life. That's why he wrote those lines.

This page intentionally left blank.

Passage IV

NATURAL SCIENCE: This passage is adapted from The Fundamental Process of Dye Chemistry by Hans Edward Fierz-David, originally published by D. Van Nostrand in 1921.

The modern dye industry is built upon the coal tar industry as its source of material, and upon the Kekule benzene theory as its scientific basis. Without these foundations, the dye industry could not have been developed.

5 The last thirty years have seen a very large increase in the number of raw materials for the dye industry, obtained by the dry distillation of coal tar. To the hydrocarbons known for a long time, such as benzene, toluene, xylene, naphthalene, and anthracene, have now been added many
10 new compounds which previously were known only in scientific circles. These compounds could not be considered for industrial application until they had been obtained in large quantity and at low cost by coal tar distillation.

Some of these newer raw materials are, for example,
15 carbazole, quinoline, pyridine, acenaphthene, pyrene, chrysene, indene, and other coal tar constituents which are now used in large quantities for the preparation of valuable dyes. Various other hydrocarbons and nitrogen-containing compounds have been placed on the market but have found
20 no industrial application as yet, although some of these may prove to be useful in the future. No uses have been found for phenanthrene, for example, although it is available in almost unlimited amounts. The homologs of benzene which are present in coal tar in only relatively small quantities
25 have also been synthesized, in recent years, from aliphatic hydrocarbons.

With the increasing demands of the dye plants, the purity of the raw materials has steadily improved, and today many of these products may be called chemically pure.
30 Modern methods have permitted the direct manufacture of pure compounds by fractional distillation and fractional crystallization. These improved techniques of the tar industry have resulted from extensive work and they constitute one of the foundations for the manufacture of intermediates for the
35 dye industry.

Generally, the supply of the necessary raw materials satisfies the demand. It is interesting to note, however, that in recent years there has been an increase in the price of
40 naphthalene, which previously was usually available in excess. This situation has arisen because changes in gas manufacture by chamber distillation have resulted in the pyrolytic decomposition of the greater part of the naphthalene present in the tar. This situation has naturally had an effect on dye intermediates derived from naphthalene.

45 The term intermediates refers to those compounds which are prepared from the original coal tar constituents by various chemical procedures and which, in turn, can be converted into commercial dyes by relatively simple further transformations. A typical example is aniline, which is
50 prepared from benzene in various ways, and which can be converted into numerous dyes.

The reactions used in the preparation of intermediates are, for the most part, simple operations. Frequently, they proceed quantitatively according to the rules of
55 stoichiometry. In other cases, side reactions are encountered which complicate the reaction and greatly reduce the yield.

It is one of the important tasks of the dye chemist to study these undesirable side reactions sufficiently to understand their nature and then, if possible, to select the
60 reaction conditions which will favor only the main reaction leading to the desired intermediate. This end is not always attained, because often the set of conditions which will eliminate the side reactions is not known, but the chemist must always bear in mind the possibility of achieving these
65 conditions by further study.

The preparation of H acid illustrates this point. This compound has been known for nearly fifty years and is still being studied extensively in many laboratories, yet to this day has not been prepared in satisfactory yield.

70 In many cases, so-called quantitative yields are obtained but the product is not a pure compound. Thus, the reaction yields the calculated quantity of product, but this is a mixture of analogous compounds which must be separated by some type of physical method. Sometimes a circuitous route can
75 be followed to arrive at an uncontaminated intermediate. For example, a substituent may be introduced and split out later. In other cases, the reactions are selected so as to prevent the formation of undesirable outcomes.

As already mentioned, the basic operations of dye
80 chemistry utilize simple chemical reactions. An intermediate can frequently be prepared in several entirely different ways and, in these cases, careful calculations must be made to determine which procedure is most advantageous. The least expensive process is often not necessarily the best
85 when other factors are taken into account. For example, the question of apparatus may enter, and calculations may show that it is uneconomical to purchase an expensive apparatus for the process if a small quantity of the material is to be produced. Furthermore, consideration must be given to the
90 usability of the side products formed. These often cannot be used at all, but may be valuable or even indispensable in another process.

In evaluating a manufacturing procedure, the apparatus in which the operations are carried out must always be considered. Unlike preparations done in the laboratory, those
95 in the plant cannot be carried out in glass equipment — except in unusual cases. Furthermore, it must be remembered that the chemicals often attack the apparatus, so its amortizement is an important consideration.

GO ON TO THE NEXT PAGE.

Most of the intermediates entering into the preparation
100 of commercial organic dyes are members of the aromatic
series. The substituents most frequently present are methyl,
halogen, nitro, amino, hydroxyl, alkoxyl, sulfo, and carboxy.
These substituents, and other less common ones, may be
introduced into the molecule either singly or in combination,
105 and their introduction may be made in various sequences
and in different manners, so that the number of possibilities
is practically unlimited. Obviously, however, practice is
governed by general principles, and the chemist who knows
the fundamentals and has a command of the methods can
110 easily determine the simplest method for preparing a desired
compound.

31. One of the main ideas established by the passage is that:

  A. it is likely that developments in the dye industry
  will result in an industrial paradigm shift.

  B. newer raw materials that are being produced are
  likely to harm the environment in unknown ways.

  C. it is significantly more important that scientific
  research be performed for the sake of gaining
  knowledge rather than for producing profit in
  industry.

  D. compounds cannot be considered for industrial use
  until they can be produced in large quantities at low
  costs.

32. According to the passage, methyl, halogen, nitro, amino,
hydroxyl, alkoxyl, sulfo, and carboxy are given as
examples of which of the following?

  F. Newer raw materials
  G. Apparatuses
  H. Substituents
  J. Homologs

33. The main purpose of the sixth paragraph (lines 45-51) is to:

  A. analyze the many reactions in which intermediates
  are present.

  B. define the term *intermediates* and provide an
  example of its use.

  C. provide a detailed list of intermediate compounds.

  D. discuss the various roles an intermediate can play in
  a reaction.

34. The passage states that modern methods have permitted
the direct manufacture of pure compounds by:

  F. preparation of H acid.
  G. chamber distillation.
  H. fractional distillation and fractional crystallization.
  J. simple operations.

35. The passage notes that H acid:

  A. is a potent "intermediate" compound with many
  industrial uses.

  B. has been known for nearly fifty years and is still
  being studied extensively.

  C. can be prepared for high quantity and quality yields.

  D. has only recently become known in scientific
  circles.

36. The word "undesirable" in line 58 most nearly means:

  F. mildly distracting.
  G. rather unfortunate.
  H. aggravating.
  J. efficiency reducing.

37. The word "attack" in line 97 most nearly means to:

  A. damage.
  B. insult.
  C. criticize.
  D. fight.

38. The passage indicates that the least expensive process is
often not necessarily the best because:

  F. it may not be the most altruistic approach to the
  formation of a given compound.

  G. it may be comparatively uneconomical when
  considering factors such as cost of the apparatus or
  usability of side products.

  H. the yield of the product might be smaller than if a
  more expensive process were to be used.

  J. an expensive process is often more likely to damage
  the product and render it inert.

39. The passage emphasizes that in evaluating the
manufacturing procedure, the apparatus must be
considered because:

  A. the procedure might be too expensive for a plant to
  consider using.

  B. preparations in the plant often cannot be performed
  in glass equipment.

  C. preparations are often confusing, and must be able
  to be performed by the layman.

  D. manufacturing plants rarely have access to the same
  chemicals that laboratories do.

40. According to the passage, aniline is an intermediate that
is prepared from which of the following chemicals?

  F. benzene
  G. pyrene
  H. phenanthrene
  J. chrysene

END OF TEST
STOP! DO NOT GO ON TO THE NEXT PAGE
UNTIL TOLD TO DO SO.

» BRAIN GOING NUMB?

- Watch out for the brain drain you may experience while slugging through four unfamiliar passages written at a college reading level on a tight timeline.

At this point, you've already pushed through over 100 questions in the English and Math tests, and if your brain isn't made of circuits and silicon, you might be getting tired.

As you read, you may get to the bottom of a paragraph and realize that you have no idea what you just read.

You may end up staring off into space or thinking far too long about one segment or question.

By practicing like you are actually taking the test, you can keep this from happening as much.

If you find yourself spacing out, you can take control.

Shift your concentration when you notice yourself zoning out. If you're having trouble with a question, **move to the next one**. If a paragraph is putting you to sleep, **skip it and move on**.

NOTES

_____

_____

_____

_____

_____

_____

_____

_____

_____

_____

_____

» INTRODUCING YOUR FRIENDLY NEIGHBORHOOD DICTIONARY

If tomorrow isn't your last chance to take the ACT, this tip could have an impact on your future ACT scores.

If tomorrow *is* the last chance, this tip could still have an impact on the rest of your education and career.

- **Use a dictionary.**

I recommend a dictionary that is written at a **high school** or **middle school** level.

Skip the collegiate stuff until you've expanded your vocabulary a bit more.

You can access great dictionaries from your smartphone on demand.

www.yourdictionary.com can be a great start.

Get yourself in the habit of doing this:

> Whenever you're reading anything for school (and even better, anything, period) look up the meaning of any word you come across that you don't understand. Check out the synonyms and derivation of the word as well.

Do this for six months, and you'll be amazed at how rarely you still have to do it and how much easier and more enjoyable it is to read.

NOTES

_____

_____

_____

_____

_____

_____

_____

_____

_____

» PLEASE READ. PRETTY PLEASE?

In the long term, nothing can help you improve your reading comprehension level and your reading speed more than reading a large number of books at your reading level.

- **Keep reading, and your reading level will go up and up.**

Compared to TV, video games, social media, and internet surfing, reading a good book is more akin to a steak dinner than an ice cream sundae.

If you force yourself to turn off the canned entertainment and dive into a book, you'll find that you start to look forward to reading.

You'll notice that your ACT Reading score will go up as well.

NOTES

_____

_____

_____

_____

_____

_____

_____

_____

_____

_____

_____

_____

_____

_____

_____

_____

» READING WRAP-UP

The ACT reading test does a good job of measuring your reading level and comprehension skills.

To the readers (and especially the bookworms) go the spoils.

That being said, if you don't have time to read the complete works of Shakespeare this week, you can still boost your scores by following the pacing and content strategies we've outlined here.

Practice reading more ACT Reading passages if you want more rehearsal in this subject area.

Our *Mastery for the ACT Reading* workbook can help you with essential vocabulary. We've listed a few resources that can help you further improve your reading scores:

ACT Reading Mini-Tests on page 222

Mastery for the ACT Reading by MasteryPrep

SnapCourse for the ACT Reading

www.FreeRice.com

www.vocabulary.com/lists/52473
(1,000 ACT vocabulary words)

NOTES

_____

_____

_____

_____

_____

_____

_____

_____

_____

» ANSWER EXPLANATIONS FOR READING PRACTICE TEST

1. **The correct answer is C.** The narrator primarily offers casual, humorous, or sarcastic remarks throughout the passage. There is no indication of genuine concern, and no details regarding the relationship the narrator had with Fyodor are provided.

2. **The correct answer is F.** Fyodor is shown to be a foolish, self-centered character throughout the passage. Additionally, there are many references made to his drunkenness. However, he is never depicted as behaving with particular cruelty.

3. **The correct answer is D.** Paragraphs one and two make no mention of Fyodor's marriages. It is not until the beginning of paragraph three that there is reference made to Fyodor's *first wife*, which may imply that he had more than one marriage.

4. **The correct answer is G.** Throughout the passage, the narrator utilizes language such as *ridiculous*, *comic*, and *ironical*, indicating that he likely finds his story to be *humorous and droll*. There is no indication made of the story being *cautionary* or *endearing*. Additionally, although the narrator does use the word *tragic*, it is apparent that the narrator is not deeply saddened by the *tragedy* he describes. *Droll* means that something is amusing in a curious or odd way.

5. **The correct answer is D.** It was not until after Adelaida left for Petersburg that Fyodor ran into the street shouting. That did not occur until Fyodor heard news of Adelaida's passing (lines 92–114).

6. **The correct answer is H.** This answer can be found in lines 64–66, which say *finally, she left the house and ran away from Fyodor Pavlovitch with a destitute divinity student.*

7. **The correct answer is D.** The word *voluptuous* means "attractive, sensual, pleasurable." A petticoat is a woman's garment. The statement is a creative way of implying that Fyodor chased after women.

8. **The correct answer is G.** The word *abhorrent* means "dislikable," while the word *preposterous* means "foolish." From the other choices, *congenial* and *amiable* mean "friendly." The words *astringent* and *pensive* mean "harsh" and "thoughtful," respectively. The word *delicate* means "soft." While *bewildering* could be accurate, implying that Fyodor was a confusing character, it is unlikely that anyone would also find Fyodor *congenial*. The details of the passage most strongly support Fyodor being considered dislikable and foolish.

9. **The correct answer is A.** This can be found directly from lines 48–50, which say *immediately after the elopement Adelaida Ivanovna discerned in a flash that she had no feeling for her husband but contempt.*

10. **The correct answer is F.** This answer can be found in lines 89–92, which say *and just at that time his wife's family received the news of her death in Petersburg. She had died quite suddenly in a garret, according to one story, of typhus, or as another version had it, of starvation.* According to the passage, Adelaida perished either from starvation or typhus.

11. The correct answer is C. Choices B and D, while possibly true, are not relevant to the passage. Choice A is tempting, but it does not pertain to the entire passage. The narrator focuses on the beginnings of these historical figures, not on their skills during the Revolutionary War. Choice C is correct as it is one of the main premises on which the passage relies.

12. The correct answer is J. The statement in line 10, *his fortune was small*, and the statement in line 12–13, *a pride which knew no shame in poverty*, are integral to discerning that the passage is referring to Samuel Adams' inability to manage his money. The other choices do not fit the meaning of this segment of the passage.

13. The correct answer is B. The author withholds any opinion regarding the fathers of the American Revolution, making choices C and D incorrect. Choice A can't be eliminated outright, but there is no evidence of a *nationalistic* (feeling of superiority of one's own country) tone given. Therefore, choice B is the best answer. *Academic* relates to scholarship, education, and learning.

14. The correct answer is F. Choice H can be eliminated since there are no details about the specific process of scalping given in the passage. Choices G and J are somewhat correct because they describe what the author wrote, but they don't get to the heart of the segment's purpose. In other words, they don't determine why the author wrote those specific lines. Choice F is the best choice since the author is showing how Putnam's experiences prepared him for the Revolutionary War that followed.

15. The correct answer is B. The tenth paragraph illustrates Washington's prowess as a soldier and leader as a young man, when *at twenty-two he fought his first battle, with forty men against five hundred and thirty, and won a victory, on its own small scale, as complete as that of Quebec* (lines 72–74). Horace Walpole is not mentioned until the following paragraph, which discusses a memoir of another man altogether, along with a quote from Washington.

16. The correct answer is J. While none of the answers pertain to each of the men mentioned in the passage, choices F, G, and H apply to at least some of them. However, there is never any mention of legal trouble in the colonies for any of the men spoken about in the passage.

17. The correct answer is A. This can be found in lines 86–89, which say *such were the men who had been reluctantly drawn by their own sense of duty, and by the urgent appeals of friends and neighbors, into the front rank of a conflict which was none of their planning.*

18. The correct answer is H. This can be found directly in lines 21–23, which state that Jefferson *worked at it after such a fashion that by thirty he was the leading lawyer of his colony.* This reveals that Jefferson dedicated himself to the practice of law.

19. The correct answer is D. Poetry, geometry, and philosophy are all mentioned as subjects of study for Nathanael Greene from lines 51–59. However, engineering is never mentioned.

20. The correct answer is G. This can be found directly from lines 77–79, which say the event *made a noise as far off as Europe, and gained for the young officer in London circles a tribute of hearty praise.* This clearly states that Washington was praised in London for his victory.

21. The correct answer is C. The words *tedious, frustrating,* and *confusing* all hold a negative connotation that is not reflected in the passage. Instead, the author speaks fondly of Emerson, his life, and his works. Therefore, choice C, *admirable*, is the best answer. *Admirable* means "respectable and excellent."

22. The correct answer is J. This can be found directly from lines 36–39, which say *he had both the leisure and the solitude to yield himself freely to the immediate impress of nature and deity, and to report the same as the true content of his life's work.* Although the concepts in the other choices are either mentioned or touched upon, only the concept of Emerson focusing on *nature and deity* as the *true content of his life's work* is focused on so clearly in the passage.

23. The correct answer is A. In the third paragraph, the author explains that the first task of the biographer is to *mark the great sweeps, the pivotal turns, the grand crises of a life, which we shall call Periods.* While this answer can be deceiving since it is not specifically describing Emerson, it provides a preface to the manner in which the biographer will approach Emerson's life. While the entire passage is about Emerson, this paragraph does not reference Emerson or his poetry. Instead, it refers to the work of the biographer in telling the story of his subject's life.

24. The correct answer is G. This answer is found in lines 57–59, which say *at the same time through this negative schooling he is slowly evolving into his positive world-view or ultimate Idea.* While F, H, and J may be partially true, the passage most strongly supports choice G.

25. The correct answer is D. This answer is found directly in lines 62–64, which say *there remains the final or Third Period of Emerson's life which he himself has indicated decisively in his poem named "Terminus."* According to the passage, the poem "Terminus" illustrates the *Third Period* in Emerson's life.

26. The correct answer is G. In context of the passage, *labyrinthine* most nearly suggests Emerson's contradictory nature. From lines 5–10, we see the author suggesting that while Emerson could, on occasion, be contradictory, as a human being he possessed a *wholeness* that defeated those contradictions.

27. The correct answer is D. Here, the author's words are not meant to be taken literally. It is most likely the case that the phrase *proclaim to the ages* is a probable reference to Emerson's creating and publishing his poetry and philosophical prose. Choice A is a literal interpretation of the lines. Choices B and C are unrelated and not indicative of the passage.

28. The correct answer is F. The context of the passage provides a clear account of how Emerson took survey of his own life. Lines 84–87, which say *remember that it is the man himself looking backward and feeling deeply the turning nodes of his spirit, who thus draws his own life-lines and marks his Periods.*

29. The correct answer is A. The context of the passage makes it clear that lines 67–68 illustrate Emerson's reflecting on his own life. Lines 73–74, which note that *in such words Emerson takes a survey of his time of life*, are meant to directly analyze the words of the poem.

30. The correct answer is H. We can find the answer by referring directly to the passage in lines 42–45, which say *then he would return to his isolated perch for fresh meditation and writing. His abode becomes for him a Castle of Defiance, also a Fortress of Liberty...* Choices F, G, and J are all found in these lines, while *his Supreme Cosmos* is not.

31. The correct answer is D. Throughout the passage, the author makes it clear that it takes a lot of effort, planning, and engineering to make certain compounds useful at an industrial level. The first instance of this appears in lines 10–13, which say *these compounds could not be considered for industrial application until they had been obtained in large quantity and at low cost by coal tar distillation.* None of the other choices appear throughout the passage.

32. The correct answer is H. This can be found directly from lines 101–103, which say *the substituents most frequently present are methyl, halogen, nitro, amino, hydroxyl, alkoxyl, sulfo, and carboxy.* This list of compounds is referred to as a group of *substituents*.

33. The correct answer is B. At the beginning of the paragraph, the term *intermediate* is defined. Additionally, *aniline* is provided as an example of an intermediate. The remaining answers do not accurately define the purpose of the sixth paragraph.

34. The correct answer is H. This can be found in lines 30–32, which say *modern methods have permitted the direct manufacture of pure compounds by fractional distillation and fractional crystallization.*

35. The correct answer is B. This can be found in lines 66–68, which say, *the preparation of H acid illustrates this point. This compound has been known for nearly fifty years and is still being studied extensively in many laboratories. . .*

36. The correct answer is J. In context of the passage, it is obvious that *undesirable* is a reference to the efficiency of the reaction. The statement in lines 55–56, which say *in other cases, side reactions are encountered which complicate the reaction and greatly reduce the yield,* supports this answer.

37. The correct answer is A. In the context of the passage, *attack* is a reference to the damaging of the apparatus. Lines 96–97, which state *furthermore, it must be remembered that the chemicals often attack the apparatus,* suggest that chemicals may be capable of causing damage to the apparatus in which they are being prepared.

38. The correct answer is G. This can be found in lines 83–88, which say *the least expensive process is often not necessarily the best when other factors are taken into account. For example, the quality of the equipment may be a factor, and calculations may show that it is uneconomical to purchase an expensive apparatus for the process if a small quantity of the material is to be produced.* The passage suggests that factors other than the cost of the process itself are also important.

39. The correct answer is B. This can be found directly from lines 92–96, which say *in evaluating a manufacturing procedure, the apparatus in which the operations are carried out must always be considered. Unlike preparations done in the laboratory, those in the plant cannot be carried out in glass equipment—except in unusual cases.* While some of the other answers may be true, they are never directly referenced in the passage.

40. The correct answer is F. This answer can be found in lines 49–51, which say *a typical example is aniline, which is prepared from benzene in various ways. . .* While the other chemicals are mentioned in the passage, none of them are spoken about in relation to aniline.

SECTION FIVE

Science

» INTRODUCTION TO THE ACT SCIENCE TEST

If you've never taken the ACT Science test, heed this warning: **It's unlikely that you've ever taken a science test similar to it.**

Not only will you be challenged with passages and questions across a variety of science subjects, but you may also find that the science knowledge you have picked up through the years isn't going to be helpful in giving your scores much of a boost.

- Only about 10% of your ACT Science score comes from what you already know, while 90% comes from what you're able to learn right then and there during the test.

- There are three essential skills we'll work on during this Boot Camp: **reading infographics, interpreting what they mean,** and **reasoning scientifically.**

NOTES

_____

_____

_____

_____

_____

_____

_____

_____

_____

_____

_____

_____

_____

_____

» SIX OR SEVEN MINI-TESTS

Don't think of the ACT Science test as a single 40-question test.

Think of it as six or seven mini-tests taken in rapid succession.

You must move through each mini-test in 5 minutes.

That includes the time you need to read through the passage and to answer the questions that go with it.

- **If you refuse to spend more than 5 minutes on any one Science passage, you'll get through the entire test without running out of time.**

It's more important that you get through the entire test than that you spend a ton of time on each of the earlier questions.

Work to move as rapidly as you can through the mini-tests in this Boot Camp and take time to consider each question.

If a question is too time-consuming, mark and move. Each passage has questions that you can answer. You just have to give yourself enough time to consider them.

There are three types of passages on the Science test:

- **Data Representation:** These passages focus mostly on reading graphs, tables, and other infographics. The questions on these passages almost never require you to read the passage. So, to finish in time, just look at the tables and graphs and then go straight to the questions. Never look back at the passage.

- **Research Summary:** These passages focus mostly on analyzing a set of experiments, which also include graphs, tables, and other infographics. The questions here only occasionally use the passage, so you should also skip the reading. However, sometimes you will need to refer back to the experiment. Don't be afraid to read if you think you need to.

- **Conflicting Viewpoints:** These will only show up once on the test. They focus on a group of theories and how they are similar or different. Even though these passages may have a graph or table, the reading portion is the most important part. So, you will have to read these to understand them. You can treat them the way you treat Reading passages: Skim and Scan.

SCIENCE TEST
35 Minutes — 40 Questions

DIRECTIONS: There are seven passages in this portion of the test. Following each passage you will be given a variety of questions. Choose the best answer to each question, then color its corresponding bubble on your answer sheet. Refer to the passages as needed. **Calculators are NOT allowed on this test.**

Passage I

Two measurements are taken of the water in a hot spring: the sulfur content and the temperature. Both of these measurements can be affected by water flow.

Sulfur content in hot springs is thought to have medicinal and therapeutic effects for those relaxing in the springs. Figure 1 shows the sulfur levels in parts per million (ppm) on 5 collection days at two different hot springs, Spring 1 and Spring 2.

Table 1 shows temperature in degrees Fahrenheit of the water in Spring 1 and Spring 2 on each of the 5 collection days. Table 2 shows the average water temperature in degrees Fahrenheit of Spring 1 and Spring 2 during this time. Figure 2 shows the water flow of each spring on the 5 collection days.

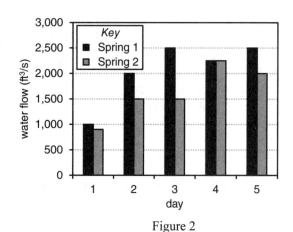

Figure 2

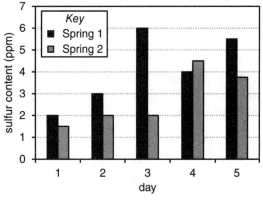

Figure 1

Table 1		
	Temperature (°F)	
Day	Spring 1	Spring 2
1	98.2	98.1
2	99.1	98.7
3	101.4	98.8
4	99.7	99.9
5	100.1	99.6

Table 2	
Spring	Average Temperature (°F)
Spring 1	99.7
Spring 2	99.0

GO ON TO THE NEXT PAGE.

1. If a sulfur content of roughly 5 ppm is considered by professionals to be the most therapeutic for visitors, which of the following collection days at which spring would have been best to visit?

   A. Day 3 at Spring 1
   B. Day 5 at Spring 1
   C. Day 1 at Spring 2
   D. Day 2 at Spring 2

2. Consider the average sulfur content and water flow at Springs 1 and 2 over the 5 collection days. Which spring had the higher average sulfur content and which spring had the higher water flow?

   Sulfur Content / Water Flow
   F. Spring 1 / Spring 1
   G. Spring 1 / Spring 2
   H. Spring 2 / Spring 1
   J. Spring 2 / Spring 2

3. According to the data, which of the following would be the most accurate description of the effect of water flow on sulfur content and temperature?

   A. As water flow increases, sulfur content increases and temperature increases.
   B. As water flow increases, sulfur content increases and temperature decreases.
   C. As water flow increases, sulfur content decreases and temperature decreases.
   D. As water flow increases, sulfur content decreases and temperature increases.

4. Which of the following is likely to be the closest to the year-round average of the temperatures of Spring 1 and Spring 2 (in degrees Fahrenheit), assuming that the average temperatures listed in Table 2 hold true year-round?

   F. 99.0°F
   G. 99.1°F
   H. 99.4°F
   J. 99.7°F

5. Suppose that on a particular day, the sulfur content of Spring 1 dropped to 1 ppm. Which of the following statements is most likely to be true?

   A. The water flow rate that day was 1,200 ft³/sec.
   B. The water flow rate that day was 500 ft³/sec.
   C. The temperature that day was 99.8°F.
   D. The temperature that day was 101.3°F.

END OF TEST
STOP! DO NOT GO ON TO THE NEXT PAGE
UNTIL TOLD TO DO SO.

» DAZED AND CONFUSED? CONNECT THE DOTS

Some of the most daunting barriers to a higher ACT score are the **confusion** and **blankness** that can set in when you try to tackle the ACT Science passages.

Most students experience having to double-check what they have read. They can end up being frustrated about not understanding the passage's meaning.

Connect the dots to avoid this pitfall.

- **Look at the graphs and pictures first.** Quickly study them.

- Then, as you read the passage, **refer back to the parts of the images that are mentioned**.

This means that you go back and forth frequently between the **passage** and its **infographics**.

- **The passage is a guide to deciphering the infographics. Read it that way.**

Complete the following exercise to help you learn how to use this strategy:

> Go back to the first Science mini-test. Draw at least 25 lines connecting words and phrases that appear in the passage with words that appear in the infographics.
>
> Then draw at least 10 lines connecting words and phrases that appear in the questions with words that appear in the infographics or passage.

Don't do this in an actual ACT test—you won't be able to read your test afterward! This is an exercise designed to help you see the connections between the passage, questions, and infographics.

Repeat the above exercise after each Science mini-test.

» CROSS OUT CONTRADICTIONS

Look at how much text is covered in a science passage.

Now consider how much text appears in the questions.

There is nearly as much to read in the questions as in the passage!

Some questions may have as many as 20 lines of text.

Eliminate some of the text to make your life easier.

- **A good way to eliminate answers is to spot contradictions.**

- A **contradiction** is a statement that can't be true because of some fact already established.

Questions that have answers which follow a format similar to "Yes, because…" or "No, because…" typically contradict *one another.*

At least a couple of these answer choices will directly contradict *the passage.*

Eliminate these contradictory answer choices, and you'll be left with a simpler decision.

For example:

3. According to the data, which of the following would be the most accurate description of the effect of water flow on sulfur content and temperature?

   A. As water flow increases, sulfur content increases and temperature increases.

   B. As water flow increases, sulfur content increases and temperature decreases.

   C. As water flow increases, sulfur content decreases and temperature decreases.

   D. As water flow increases, sulfur content decreases and temperature increases.

We can clearly see in Figure 2 that water flow is higher on Day 5 than Day 1. We can also see that sulfur content is higher on Day 5 than Day 1. For that reason, choices C and D contradict the passage and so can be eliminated. Sulfur content did not decrease as water flow increased.

Because one part of the answer contradicts the passage, none of it is true.

Instead of trying to consider all of the passage and answer choices at once, break them down into their component parts and work on it from there.

» READING GRAPHS

- **Your first task when you start a Science passage is to read the graphs, charts, and infographics.**

You've already started doing this with the *connect the dots* technique. While you're first reading the graphs, follow these tips to maximize your time.

Look immediately to the **x- and y-axis labels** (the horizontal and vertical lines, respectively).

Look at the **image** in the main part of the graph, and look for **labels** there.

The chart may contain two *y*-axes or two *x*-axes. That means that the quantities being graphed on the same axis are directly proportional: as one increases, so does the other.

Give yourself about 15 seconds to look over these figures and tables.

Try to check your understanding of the graph by reading one of the values it describes and observing any trends you can detect as you move from left to right across the *x*-axis.

Try this with the next passage and see if it helps you better understand what you are reading. Continue reading the test in this manner for the remainder of these mini-tests.

NOTES

_____

_____

_____

_____

_____

_____

_____

_____

_____

_____

This page intentionally left blank.

Passage II

Three metal alloys contain varying levels of chromium, which helps prevent the process of corrosion due to oxidation, commonly called rust. When rust forms on metals, hydroxide ions are produced as a by-product.

Table 1 shows the volume of OH^- ions produced over time from samples of three metal alloys with varying chromium content.

The trial for the first metal alloy was then repeated four times, each time with one of four different corrosion inhibitors at a constant concentration. The results of the trials are shown below in Figure 1.

Table 1					
		Concentration of ions [OH^-] produced (μM)			
Metal alloy	Chromium content (%)	Day 2	Day 4	Day 6	Day 8
1	9.0	19	42	86	131
2	10.5	2	4	8	12
3	11.0	1	3	5	7

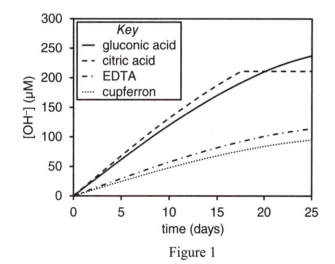

Figure 1

6. Based on Table 1, which of the following graphs best shows how the volume of OH^- produced by Metal Alloy 3 changed over time?

F.
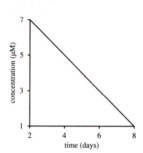

G.
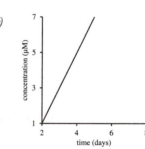

H.
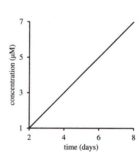

J.
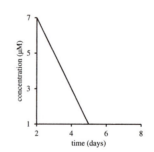

7. Based on Table 1, if the volume of OH^- produced by Day 10 from the Metal Alloy 2 sample had been measured, it would most likely have been:

A. less than 12 mL.
B. between 12 and 22 mL.
C. between 22 and 34 mL.
D. greater than 34 mL.

GO ON TO THE NEXT PAGE.

8. According to Table 1, what volume of OH⁻ was produced by Metal Alloy 1 from the time the volume was measured on Day 4 until the time the volume was measured on Day 6?

F. 16 mL
G. 24 mL
H. 44 mL
J. 62 mL

9. According to Figure 1, which of the following corrosion inhibitors was most effective at preventing Metal Alloy 1 from rusting?

A. gluconic acid
B. citric acid
C. EDTA
D. cupferron

10. Consider the volume of OH⁻ produced on Day 4 by the Metal Alloy 1 sample that contained no corrosion inhibitors. According to Table 1 and Figure 1, the Metal Alloy 1 sample containing cupferron produced approximately the same volume of OH⁻ on which of the following days?

F. Day 3
G. Day 5
H. Day 9
J. Day 11

END OF TEST
STOP! DO NOT GO ON TO THE NEXT PAGE
UNTIL TOLD TO DO SO.

» SHOW ME THE DATA

Here are a few tips to consider when your answer choices are all graphs:

You don't have to spend the time making your own detailed graph in order to get these questions right.

- **First look at the differences between the choices.** Perhaps two are increasing while two are decreasing.

- **Then look at the line characteristics.** Are they all straight? Does one or more curve? Do any have a steep drop-off after a point?

- **Eliminate the choices that CAN'T describe the answer to the question** because they are moving in the wrong direction, etc.

- Usually there will only be one choice left: *the right one!*

Let's look at an example question to see how this works.

6. Based on Table 1, which of the following graphs best shows how the volume of OH⁻ produced by Metal Alloy 3 changed over time?

F.
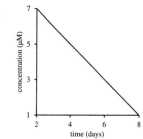

H.
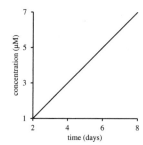

G.
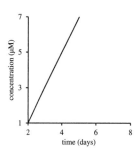

J.
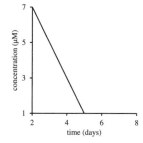

Since the OH⁻ production increases from Day 2 to Day 8, we can eliminate choices F and J (they show a decreasing slope). Now we are left with two choices instead of four. The question then becomes whether we should choose a graph with a steep upward slope or one with a more gradual slope. Since the OH⁻ production reaches only 7μM by Day 8, H is a more accurate graph and is the best answer choice.

Simplify your task on data representation questions by eliminating the answers that don't match the characteristics of the data.

NOTES

Passage III

A group of students studied force by using two identical force-meters, Meter A and Meter B, as shown in Figure 1.

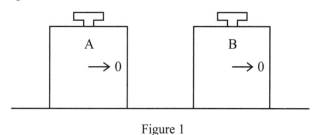

Figure 1

When a force (such as weight, or *mass multiplied by gravity*) was exerted on the surface of the meter, the hand rotated counterclockwise on the dial. The amount of the rotation was directly proportional to the strength of the force.

Study 1

Before each of the Trials 1-3, the students set the dial readings of both Meters A and B to zero. In each of these 3 trials, Meter A was stacked on top of Meter B. In Trial 1, no weight was placed on Meter A; in Trial 2, a 3.0 Newton (N) weight was placed on the platform of Meter A; and in Trial 3, a 6.0 N weight was placed on the platform of Meter A. The results of these trials are shown below in Figure 2.

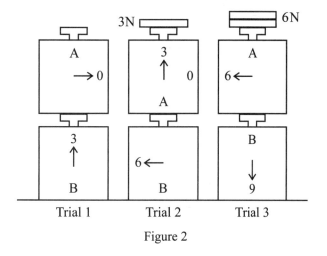

Figure 2

Study 2

The students then positioned a bridge on top of the two meters so that exactly 1 m of bridge length rested between Meter A and Meter B. Before each of the Trials 4-6, the students set the dial readings of Meters A and B to zero. This is shown in Figure 3.

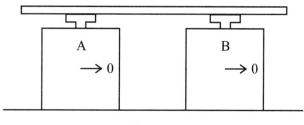

Figure 3

In each of these 3 trials, the center of a 6.0 N weight was placed on the bridge at various distances from the edge of Meter A. In Trial 4, the weight was .125 m from the edge; in Trial 5, the weight was .25 m from the edge; and in Trial 6, the weight was .375 m from the edge. The results of these trials are shown in Figure 4.

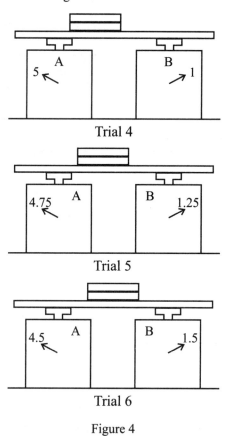

Figure 4

GO ON TO THE NEXT PAGE.

11. In which of the Trials in Study 2 was the force of the 6.0 N weight equally distributed between the two meters?

    A. Trial 4
    B. Trial 5
    C. Trial 6
    D. None of the trials

12. Based on the results from Study 1, Meters A and B each must weigh:

    F. 0.0 N.
    G. 3.0 N.
    H. 6.0 N.
    J. 9.0 N.

13. In Study 2, as the distance of the 6.0 N weight from the edge of Meter B increased, the force placed on Meter A:

    A. increased.
    B. decreased.
    C. remained the same.
    D. changed without uniformity.

14. Which of the following statements most likely describes why it was important to set Meters A and B to zero before beginning the Study 2 trials?

    F. It was important to include the weight of the scale.
    G. It was important to include the weight of the bridge.
    H. It was important to discount the weight of the bridge.
    J. The meters become unreliable over time.

15. Suppose that in a new study, Meter B has a 3.0 N weight placed on top of it, and Meter A is then placed upside down on top of that weight. Which of the following graphics best represents the results of such an arrangement?

    A.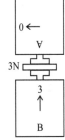

    B.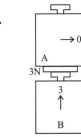

    C.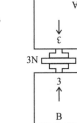

    D.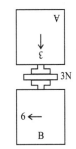

16. According to Trial 6, what was the weight being placed on Meter B by the 6.0 N weight?

    F. 1.5 N
    G. 3.0 N
    H. 4.5 N
    J. 6.0 N

END OF TEST

STOP! DO NOT GO ON TO THE NEXT PAGE
UNTIL TOLD TO DO SO.

» THE SCIENTIFIC METHOD IN FIVE MINUTES

Scientists use the scientific method in order to learn about the world around them.

They ask **questions**, do background **research**, create **hypotheses**, test those hypotheses by doing **experiments**, **analyze** results, draw **conclusions**, and **communicate** findings.

- **During an experiment, it's important that scientists control it in such a way to actually answer their initial question.**

For example, if you wanted to know how sleep affects test scores but didn't make sure that your subject slept the correct amount for your experiment or didn't keep them from taking a nap right before the test, then your experiment would be invalid.

- **In an experiment, scientists want to change only the things that they are measuring and learning about.**

- **Scientists want to eliminate any other cause of change so that their conclusions are valid.**

For example, in this question:

14. Which of the following statements most likely describes why it was important to set Meters A and B to zero before beginning the Study 2 trials?

F. It was important to include the weight of the scale.

G. It was important to include the weight of the bridge.

H. It was important to discount the weight of the bridge.

J. The meters become unreliable over time.

The experiment will be affected if the weight of the bridge isn't controlled. By setting the scales to zero after placing the bridge on them, the bridge's weight can't affect the results of the experiment. Setting the scale to zero eliminates the measurement of the weight of the scale or bridge, so that means you can eliminate choices F and G. Also, choice J, while possible, is extremely unlikely and not supported anywhere in the passage. Therefore, choice H is your best answer.

Sometimes you can simplify this type of question by asking yourself, **"Why did the scientists do this? How could their decision to do this improve their results?"**

» KEEP IT SIMPLE

The reading and science passages are the ones most likely to cause overthinking.

It's important to **KISS – keep it simple, science.**

If an answer describes something that was never talked about in the passage or infographics, chances are that it is wrong.

Don't trick yourself into picking a wrong answer.

Let's look again at question 14 to illustrate this point:

14. Which of the following statements most likely describes why it was important to set Meters A and B to zero before beginning the Study 2 trials?

    F. It was important to include the weight of the scale.

    G. It was important to include the weight of the bridge.

    H. It was important to discount the weight of the bridge.

    J. The meters become unreliable over time.

Choice J is sometimes selected incorrectly because there's nothing in the passage that says the meters won't become unreliable over time.

That being said, there is nothing that even suggests that they *will* become unreliable. Don't overthink it! If choice J were the correct answer, the test writers would have mentioned meters becoming unreliable. They're not allowed to write test questions that are that vague.

Be skeptical of the answer choices.

If you're tempted to choose an explanation, ask yourself, **"Does this really explain why the scientists did this?"**

Until you find a satisfactory answer, don't try to make a square peg fit into a round hole.

Passage IV

The octane rating of fuel is a measure of how smoothly it burns in an internal combustion engine. Fuels with a lower octane rating knock (explode) when burned, which lowers efficiency and potentially causes damage to the engine. Heptane knocks frequently when burned and is given an octane rating of 0, while isooctane burns very smoothly with little to no knocking and is given an octane rating of 100.

Different mixtures of heptane and isooctane are combined in order to obtain several mixtures of fuels with octane ratings between 0 and 100. The results are listed below in Table 1.

Experiment 1

A sample of each of the fuel mixtures listed in Table 1 was burned in an engine at a speed of 500 revolutions per minute (rpm) so that an octane rating could be assigned to the listed fuels by measuring the number of knocks per minute.

Table 1		
Volume of heptane (mL)	Volume of isooctane (mL)	Octane rating
0	100	100
20	80	80
35	65	65
50	50	50
85	15	15
100	0	0

Experiment 2

In order to increase the octane rating, tetraethyllead (TEL) was added to 1,000 mL samples of isooctane. Each of the fuel mixtures listed in Table 1 was tested in this way. The results are shown below in Figure 1.

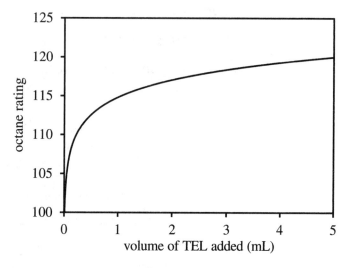

Figure 1

Experiment 3

The minimum octane rating of a fuel required for an engine to run without damage is known as the *engine octane requirement* (EOR). Two fuels (A and B) were burned in separate, but identical, engines at varying speeds. The resulting octane ratings of the fuels and the EOR of the engines at these varying speeds are shown below in Table 2.

Table 2			
Engine speed (rpm)	EOR	Octane rating	
		Fuel A	Fuel B
1,000	98.3	97.9	98.6
1,500	97.8	97.8	98.2
2,000	96.1	96.9	97.8
2,500	94.2	95.2	96.7
3,000	91.5	93.6	94.3

GO ON TO THE NEXT PAGE.

17. Based on Table 1, if 3 mL of heptane were mixed with 7 mL of isooctane, the octane rating of this mixture at 500 rpm would be which of the following?

    A. 3
    B. 7
    C. 30
    D. 70

18. According to Experiment 3, as engine rpm increases, the EOR:

    F. decreases.
    G. increases.
    H. decreases, then increases.
    J. increases, then decreases.

19. Based on Experiment 2 and Table 1, if 4 mL of TEL were added to a mixture of 800 mL of isooctane and 200 mL of heptane, what would be the most likely octane rating of the resulting fuel?

    A. Less than 50
    B. Between 50 and 80
    C. Between 80 and 120
    D. Greater than 120

20. Suppose a trial had been performed during Experiment 3 at a speed of 2,250 rpm. Given this speed, which of the following octane ratings would most likely be accurate for Fuel A and Fuel B?

    Fuel A / Fuel B
    F. 96.9 / 97.8
    G. 95.2 / 96.7
    H. 97.4 / 98.1
    J. 96.0 / 96.9

21. Which of the following expressions describes the octane rating of the fuel mixtures in Table 1 (where V is volume in mL)?

    A. $\dfrac{100\left(V_{isooctane} + V_{heptane}\right)}{\left(V_{isooctane} + V_{heptane}\right)}$

    B. $\dfrac{100\left(V_{isooctane}\right)}{\left(V_{isooctane} + V_{heptane}\right)}$

    C. $\dfrac{100\left(V_{heptane}\right)}{\left(V_{isooctane} + V_{heptane}\right)}$

    D. $\dfrac{100\left(V_{isooctane}\right)}{\left(V_{heptane}\right)}$

22. In Experiment 3, assuming that the engine will remain functional at speeds between 1,000 rpm and 3,000 rpm, which of the two fuels would be better for the engine to use?

    F. Fuel A, because it has an octane rating higher than the EOR for all engine speeds.
    G. Fuel A, because it has an octane rating lower than the EOR for all engine speeds.
    H. Fuel B, because it has an octane rating higher than the EOR for all engine speeds.
    J. Fuel B, because it has an octane rating lower than the EOR for all engine speeds.

GO ON TO THE NEXT PAGE.

Passage V

The universe is thought to be roughly 14 billion years old, having begun in a flash with an event known as the Big Bang. Our universe is composed of the totality of time, space, and matter, containing roughly 100 billion galaxies, each of which contains roughly 100 billion stars. Observations have shown that the universe is currently expanding at an accelerating rate, causing all of its galaxies, including our Milky Way, to quickly move away from each other. There are several competing theories on the ultimate fate of the universe, though none of them are yet agreed upon by the scientific community at large.

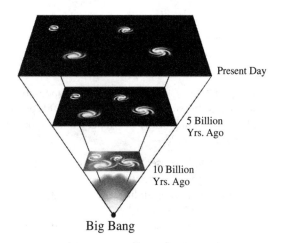

Figure 1

Two scientists present their viewpoints about how the universe will end.

Scientist A

The universe will end in what is known as the Big Freeze, where the accelerating expansion of the universe eventually causes the temperature of the universe to approach absolute zero. As the expansion of the universe will continue on forever, the entropy of the universe will increase at a rapid rate. The universe will grow darker and darker until there is no longer enough gas for stars to continue forming. At this time, the universe will only be populated by black holes, which will eventually die as well. After trillions of years of slowly fading out, the universe will die in a heat death, meaning that it will have exhausted all of the free thermodynamic energy remaining, preventing any work from being done and preventing all of the processes necessary for creating or sustaining life from continuing.

Scientist B

The universe will not end with the Big Freeze, but instead with the Big Crunch. Even though the universe is currently expanding at an accelerating rate, this expansion is not unlimited. The expansion speed will not exceed the escape velocity to allow expansion to extend beyond a universal event horizon. The gravitational attraction of all of the matter in the universe will cause it to eventually begin retracting and rubber-banding backwards. This is not dissimilar to the same elliptical path by which heavenly bodies rotate around each other, hurtling away and then being dragged back by gravitational pull. In this way, the universe will not end in a heat death, but will eventually collapse back in on itself, resulting in the reformation of the universe with another Big Bang.

GO ON TO THE NEXT PAGE.

23. Consistent with Scientist A's position, over time entropy in a closed system is known to increase. According to the laws of thermodynamics, this means that a closed system will eventually exhaust all of the free energy capable of performing work it contains. If Scientist A were to use this aspect of thermodynamics to support his position, how might Scientist B attempt to refute it?

A. By suggesting that the Universe is not finite, but is instead infinite and therefore cannot be a closed system.

B. By stating that stars have only a limited life span.

C. By suggesting that gravitational force will prevent the Universe from exceeding escape velocity.

D. By saying that dark energy fuels the acceleration of the Universe's expansion.

24. Critical density is the value that determines whether or not the Universe will begin to contract before reaching escape velocity. Scientist A is most likely to say which of the following?

F. Critical density is high enough to cause the Universe to contract.

G. Critical density is not high enough to cause the Universe to contract.

H. Critical density does not determine whether or not the Universe will contract.

J. The Universe will reach escape velocity and then contract.

25. Which of the following statements will Scientists A and B most likely agree on?

A. The Universe will contract before reaching escape velocity.

B. The Universe will reach escape velocity.

C. The Universe is expanding.

D. The Big Bang did not occur.

26. Suppose it is discovered that the rate of the expansion of the Universe is decreasing. Which Scientist's position would this most likely support?

F. Scientist A

G. Scientist B

H. Both Scientists A and B

J. Neither Scientists A nor B

27. The Andromeda Galaxy and the Milky Way Galaxy are set to collide with one another in roughly 4 billion years. Does this fact argue for or against Scientist A's position, or neither?

A. It argues for Scientist A's position because the Universe's accelerating expansion causes the galaxies to expand into one another.

B. It argues against Scientist A's position because the galaxies could not collide in a Universe that is expanding at an accelerated rate.

C. Neither; the two galaxies may be attracting one another faster than the Universe is expanding.

D. Neither; the two galaxies will not collide with one another.

28. If Scientist A's position is correct, what is most likely to occur nearing the end of the Universe's life?

F. The Universe will have shrunk to an extremely small, dense singularity.

G. The Universe will have expanded to trillions of times its current size, with nearly no entropy.

H. The Universe will have expanded to trillions of times its current size, with nearly zero free energy.

J. The Universe will be producing more stars than it is today.

29. If Scientist B's position is correct, what is most likely to occur nearing the end of the Universe's life?

A. The Universe will have shrunk to an extremely small, dense singularity.

B. The Universe will have expanded to trillions of times its current size, with nearly no entropy.

C. The Universe will have expanded to trillions of times its current size, with nearly no free energy.

D. The Universe's critical density will have become nearly nonexistent.

GO ON TO THE NEXT PAGE.

» THE NO-GRAPH PASSAGE

There will always be one passage that has either no graphic or a graphic that does not help much in answering the questions.

These passages compare two studies or two scientific opinions.

Unlike the other science passages, the key to solving these questions is in the **passage** and not the infographics.

From the onset, try to understand the **similarities** and **differences** between the two opinions or studies described.

- **Most of the questions will concern comparison and contrast.**

- **Pay particular attention to how the scientists contradict one another.**

It can help to imagine that the two scientists are on a split screen arguing on a news show. Try reading a few lines of each scientist's information at a time, instead of all of Scientist A, then all of Scientist B. This will help clarify the difference between the two scientists' opinions.

Typically, the descriptions of each scientist's opinion follow the same sequence, so if you bounce back and forth you can easily compare the scientists' takes on the various subtopics in the passage.

Here is an exercise designed to help you dissect this question type:

Write down three similarities and three differences between the two scientists' opinions in Passage V.

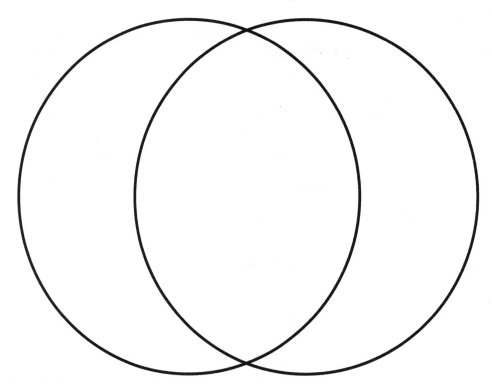

» TWO RIGHT ANSWERS

If two answers seem equally correct, then chances are neither of them is the right answer.

For example, in this question:

28. If Scientist A's position is correct, what is most likely to occur nearing the end of the Universe's life?

    F. The Universe will have shrunk to an extremely small, dense singularity.

    G. The Universe will have expanded to trillions of times its current size, with nearly no entropy.

    H. The Universe will have expanded to trillions of times its current size, with nearly zero free energy.

    J. The Universe will be producing more stars than it is today.

If F is correct and the Universe is shrinking, then there would also be more star production as stated in choice J. One follows the other logically. For that reason, neither is correct.

During the Science test, you might find yourself weighing two distinct scientific possibilities and trying to figure out which one is more likely. If one possibility causes more than one answer choice to be correct, it's not the right possibility. Go with the other one.

ACT tests are built so that only one answer is correct for each question.

Passage VI

High-salt environments cause blueberry bushes to grow poorly. This is caused by two distinct processes:

- An increased concentration of Na^+ ions in the cytoplasm
- A decreased H_2O absorption by the plant cells

Arabidopsis thaliana, a small flowering plant, carries the gene AtNHXI, whose product, VAC, increases the uptake and removal of Na^+.

A group of researchers bred four identical lines of blueberry bushes (B_1-B_4). They then isolated the AtNHXI gene from the *Arabidopsis thaliana* and inserted two copies of this gene into the B_1 genome. They repeated this process for B_2 and B_3, changing the AtNHXI alleles for each so that B_1, B_2, and B_3 had distinct AtNHXI genotypes. They then performed an experiment involving the growth of these lines.

Experiment

Seedlings from each of the lines were planted and allowed to grow in 10 L nutrient solutions in which 2 grams of NaCl were added. After 90 days of growth, the researchers recorded the average height, average mass, and average berry mass of the different lines. The results of their findings are recorded in Table 1.

The researchers repeated this process, increasing the grams of NaCl to 8. The results of their findings are recorded in Table 2.

The researchers then repeated this process a final time, increasing the grams of NaCl to 64. The results of their findings are recorded in Table 3.

Table 1			
2 g NaCl / 10 L Nutrient Solution			
Line	Height (cm)	Mass (kg)	Berry mass (g)
B_1	60.9	0.7	0.80
B_2	61.2	0.7	0.81
B_3	59.8	0.7	0.79
B_4	60.4	0.7	0.80

Table 2			
8 g NaCl / 10 L Nutrient Solution			
Line	Height (cm)	Mass (kg)	Berry mass (g)
B_1	58.5	0.6	0.75
B_2	59.6	0.6	0.77
B_3	42.3	0.4	0.51
B_4	40.6	0.4	0.49

Table 3			
64 g NaCl / 10 L Nutrient Solution			
Line	Height (cm)	Mass (kg)	Berry mass (g)
B_1	58.3	0.6	0.74
B_2	58.9	0.6	0.78
B_3	21.2	0.2	0.00
B_4	20.5	0.2	0.00

GO ON TO THE NEXT PAGE.

30. The researchers included a control specimen in order to ensure accuracy. Which of the four lines, B_1-B_4, was most likely the control?

    F. B_1

    G. B_2

    H. B_3

    J. B_4

31. For each line of blueberry bushes, as NaCl concentration increases, plant height:

    A. decreases.

    B. increases.

    C. decreases or increases.

    D. stays the same.

32. One blueberry plant produced the largest average berry mass at .81 grams. Which of the following best describes this plant?

    F. B_1 in 10 L of solution containing 64 g of NaCl

    G. B_1 in 10 L of solution containing 8 g of NaCl

    H. B_2 in 10 L of solution containing 2 g of NaCl

    J. B_2 in 10 L of solution containing 8 g of NaCl

33. Which of the following was an independent variable in the experiment?

    A. Blueberry mass

    B. Blueberry bush height

    C. Amount of nutrient solution

    D. Insertion of AtNHXI

34. The lines B_1-B_3 received varying amounts of influence from the AtNHXI gene with respect to NaCl presence. Which of the following best describes what may have occurred with the insertion of this gene into the lines?

    F. B_1-B_3 all received the same resistance to the presence of NaCl in the solution.

    G. B_1 and B_2 received resistance to the presence of NaCl in the solution, but B_3 did not.

    H. B_1 and B_3 received resistance to the presence of NaCl in the solution, but B_2 did not.

    J. B_1-B_3 did not receive any resistance to the presence of NaCl in the solution.

35. Suppose that the data for these blueberry bush lines is plotted on a graph with berry mass on the x-axis and height on the y-axis. Suppose also that a line of best fit is found for each of these blueberry bushes. Which of the following would characterize the slope of these best fit lines most accurately?

    A. The lines would have a positive slope.

    B. The lines would have a negative slope.

    C. The lines would have a zero slope.

    D. The lines would have an undefined slope.

GO ON TO THE NEXT PAGE.

Passage VII

A copper rod is heated on one end by a heat source (shown in Figure 1). A student begins a timer at the moment one end of the copper rod reaches 100° Celsius. He measures the time it takes the cool end of the copper rod, which begins at room temperature, to reach the temperature of the heat source. The results are recorded below in Figure 2.

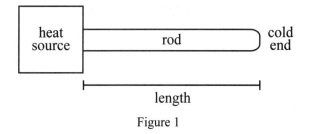

Figure 1

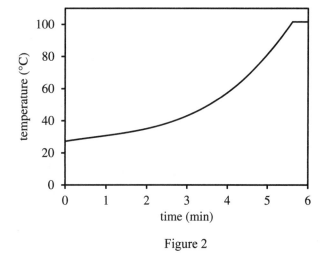

Figure 2

The student then removes the heat source from the now uniformly heated copper rod and records time it takes for the entire copper rod to return to room temperature. The results are recorded below in Figure 3.

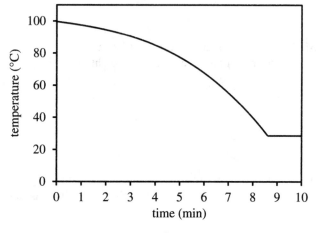

Figure 3

GO ON TO THE NEXT PAGE.

36. According to Figure 2, at what time does the initially cool end of the copper rod match the temperature of the heated end of the copper rod?

    F.   3.5 min
    G.   4.5 min
    H.   5.5 min
    J.   8.5 min

37. According to Figure 3, how long does it take for the uniformly heated rod to return to room temperature?

    A.   6.5 min
    B.   7.5 min
    C.   8.5 min
    D.   9.5 min

38. Which of the following is unlikely to affect the time it takes the opposite end of the copper rod to reach the same temperature as the end adjoining the heat source?

    F.   rod length
    G.   rod width
    H.   rod temperature
    J.   whichever end of the rod is placed adjoining the heat source when the experiment starts

39. If the student were to remove the heat source from the end of the rod at 2 ½ minutes and keep the heat source away for a total of 5 minutes before returning it to the rod, which of the following is most likely to be the time at which the cool end of the rod reaches the temperature of the heated end of the rod (including the time already elapsed)?

    A.   Less than 10 minutes
    B.   Exactly 10 minutes
    C.   More than 10 minutes
    D.   This cannot be determined.

40. Which of the following arrangements of identical copper rods is most likely to take the least time to bring to a uniformly heated temperature with a heat source?

    F.

    G.

    H.

    J.

END OF TEST
STOP! DO NOT GO ON TO THE NEXT PAGE
UNTIL TOLD TO DO SO.

» SCIENCE WRAP-UP

Remember to treat the ACT Science test like **seven mini-tests**, not a single daunting one.

Do this, and you'll manage your time much better and have a chance to get through the entire test.

- **Don't overthink** the science questions.

- **Use the infographics** to find the answers that you need.

- **Spot contradictions** to narrow down your choices.

ADDITIONAL STUDY

If you feel you need more practice in this area, start with the ACT Science Mini-Tests on page 232. After that, I recommend that you pick up the *Mastery for the ACT Science* workbook as well as the *Real ACT Prep Guide, 3rd Edition* and work through the science passages they contain. Pay special attention to dissecting the infographics.

Additionally, you might want to pick up magazines such as *Scientific American*, *Popular Science*, and *National Geographic*. Reading articles from these magazines can help improve your stamina during the ACT test.

NOTES

_____

_____

_____

_____

_____

_____

_____

_____

_____

_____

_____

» ANSWER EXPLANATIONS FOR SCIENCE PRACTICE TEST

1. **The correct answer is B.** View the data from Figure 1. The best answer is the day and spring that has sulfur content closest to 5 ppm. Of the answers listed, the one that appears to be closest to 5 ppm is Spring 1 on Day 5.

2. **The correct answer is F.** According to Figures 1 and 2, of the two springs, Spring 1 has both the greater average sulfur content and the greater average water flow.

3. **The correct answer is A.** Look at the data from Table 1 and Figures 1 and 2. On days with high water flow, temperature and sulfur content appear to increase. On days with low water flow, temperature and sulfur content appear to decrease. This means that when water flow increases, temperature and sulfur content increase, too.

4. **The correct answer is H.** The question asks to find the year-round average temperature of the two springs. Because Spring 1 has an average temperature of 99.7 degrees and Spring 2 has an average temperature of 99.0 degrees, the average of the two should be roughly halfway between these two values. The closest answer is 99.4 degrees Fahrenheit.

5. **The correct answer is B.** A sulfur content of 1 ppm should correspond to a relatively low water flow rate and temperature. We can estimate that the water flow and temperature levels should be lower than those corresponding to Spring 2's measurements on the first day (which had sulfur content levels of 1.5 ppm). Of the answers listed, the only relatively low value is a flow rate of 500 ft^3/sec. 1,200 ft^3/sec corresponds more closely to a sulfur content of 2 ppm. The temperatures 99.8°F and 101.3°F corresponded to sulfur contents of 4 and 6 ppm in this experiment, respectively. Therefore, a water flow rate of 500 ft^3/sec is the best choice.

6. **The correct answer is H.** On Day Zero, 0 mL of OH$^-$ will have been produced. By Day 8, however, 7 mL of OH$^-$ will have been produced. Therefore, choice H is the best answer. The other graphs either have negative slopes or grow too quickly.

7. **The correct answer is B.** By Day 2, Metal Alloy 2 has produced 2 mL of OH$^-$ and by Day 4 it has produced 4 mL of OH$^-$, an increase of 2 mL. By Day 6, there is an increase of 4 mL and by Day 8, an additional increase of 4 mL. It is most likely that, by Day 10, there will have been an additional increase between 4 and 8 mL of OH$^-$, placing the total OH$^-$ produced between 12 and 22 mL.

8. **The correct answer is H.** The difference between the mL OH$^-$ produced on Day 6 and the mL OH$^-$ produced on Day 4 is 86–42 = 44 mL. Therefore, 44 mL of OH$^-$ were produced between Day 4 and Day 6.

9. **The correct answer is D.** Rusting produces hydroxide ions as a byproduct. So, lower hydroxide production implies that less rusting has occurred. Metal Alloy 1 with a cupferron coating produced the smallest amount of OH$^-$.

10. **The correct answer is H.** On Day 4, Metal Alloy 1 had produced 42 mL of OH$^-$. According to Figure 1, Metal Alloy 1, when coated with cupferron, instead takes approximately 9 days to produce this amount of OH$^-$.

11. **The correct answer is D.** In all of the trials, the weight is placed closer to Meter A than Meter B. Since there is 1 m of length between meters A and B, the center of the weight

would need to be placed exactly 0.5 m from the edge in order for the weight to be evenly distributed between the two meters.

12. **The correct answer is G.** According to the passage, Meters A and B are identical. In Study 1, we see that a 3.0 N weight causes the dial to rotate the same amount as the weight of one of the meters. This implies that Meters A and B both weigh 3.0 N.

13. **The correct answer is A.** As the weight is moved farther away from Meter B's edge and closer to Meter A's edge, the force of the weight becomes more distributed to Meter A than to Meter B. This causes the force exerted on Meter A to increase as the weight's distance from Meter B increases.

14. **The correct answer is H.** The meters were set to zero after the bridge was placed on top of them, which was done in order to discount the weight of the bridge from Trials 4–6. The weight of the bridge was discounted to produce meaningful results about the distribution of the force of the 6.0 N weight.

15. **The correct answer is D.** Meter B, facing upward would have the force of the 3.0 N weight and the force of Meter A exerted upon it, meaning that Meter B should read 6.0 N. Meter A, upside down, has no force exerted upon it by the weight nor by Meter A. However, it is exerting its own weight on its own scale, meaning that it would be reading 3.0 N.

16. **The correct answer is F.** Meter B reads 1.5 N during Trial 6 in Figure 4.

17. **The correct answer is D.** According to Table 1, the octane rating is equivalent to the percent of isooctane in the mixture. Because isooctane makes up 7/10 of the mixture, the octane rating of this mixture is 70.

18. **The correct answer is F.** Look at the data in Table 2. Each time rpm increases, EOR decreases. There is no increase in rpm that causes the EOR to increase.

19. **The correct answer is C.** From Figure 1, we see that varying amounts of TEL between 0 and 1 mL increases octane rating from 100 to 120, but additional TEL does not increase octane rating beyond 120. The mixture in question has an octane rating of 80. We can reasonably hypothesize that TEL will cause an 80 octane rating mixture to increase in octane rating, but it is unlikely that it will increase beyond an octane rating of 120.

20. **The correct answer is J.** The octane ratings for Fuels A and B for an engine rpm of 2,250 will most likely fall between the octane ratings of Fuels A and B at 2,000 and 2,500 rpm. Fuel A has an octane rating of 96.9 at 2,000 rpm and an octane rating of 95.2 at 2,500 rpm. Fuel B has an octane rating of 97.8 at 2,000 rpm and an octane rating of 96.7 at 2,500 rpm.

21. **The correct answer is B.** In Table 1, the octane rating is the percent of the isooctane in the solution. Octane rating is found by dividing the volume of isooctane by the sum of the volumes of the isooctane and heptane and then multiplying this value by 100. For example, a mixture of 50 mL of isooctane and 50 mL of heptane gives 100(50)/(50+50) = 100(1/2) = 50.

22. **The correct answer is H.** EOR is described as the minimum octane rating required for a fuel to be acceptable in an engine. According to Table 2, at 1,000 rpm, Fuel A's octane rating falls below the minimum octane rating required by the engine. Therefore, Fuel B, which never has an octane rating fall below the minimum requirement, is the better choice.

23. **The correct answer is A.** This is the only answer that addresses the point raised by Scientist A. Scientist A's point is dependent on the Universe being a 'closed system.' In choice A,

Scientist B offers a response that would invalidate Scientist A's claim. Each of the other answers does not do this.

24. **The correct answer is G.** By definition, critical density is the density at which the Universe would not reach escape velocity and continue to indefinitely expand. Scientist A's position is that the Universe will expand at an accelerating rate without ceasing. Therefore, he would suggest that the Universe does not have the critical density necessary to prevent the Universe from reaching escape velocity.

25. **The correct answer is C.** Both scientists agree that the Universe is indeed expanding. What they do not agree on is whether the Universe will continue to expand or will expand for some unknown time and then begin to contract.

26. **The correct answer is G.** If it is discovered that the rate of expansion of the Universe is decreasing, this might suggest that the Universe is beginning to decelerate and contract, supporting the position of Scientist B only.

27. **The correct answer is C.** Even though in an expanding Universe all galaxies are moving away from each other at increasing speeds, this does not necessarily mean that two galaxies cannot also be moving toward one another at a faster rate, due to the greater force of gravity between the two entities. Therefore, it is possible for the Universe to be expanding and for the Milky Way and Andromeda to be colliding, simultaneously.

28. **The correct answer is H.** According to Scientist A's position, the Universe is expanding at an increasing rate, and it will continue to do so indefinitely. This process will cause all of the free energy of the Universe to eventually convert to entropy, causing a state where no new stars can be born, and where there is nearly no free energy left in the Universe.

29. **The correct answer is A.** According to Scientist B's position, the Universe will continue to expand for some time, but it will eventually contract and collapse back in on itself. In this case, it is most likely that all of the matter in the Universe will collapse into one very small, dense point called a singularity.

30. **The correct answer is J.** According to the passage, B_1-B_3 were given some version of the AtNXHI gene. B_4 was not genetically altered for the experiment. This was the control specimen.

31. **The correct answer is A.** Look at the information given in Tables 1-3. As NaCl concentration increases from Experiments 1 to 3, height decreases from Experiments 1 to 3. Therefore, as NaCl concentration increases, height decreases.

32. **The correct answer is H.** The final column of each table lists the average blueberry mass of each plant, in grams. We see that the largest value in this column is in Table 1, at 0.81 grams. This is B_2 in 10 L of solution with 2 g of NaCl.

33. **The correct answer is D.** The only independent variable listed is the insertion of the AtNXHI gene. The amount of nutrient solution is held constant, and the blueberry bush height and blueberry mass are dependent variables which vary based on NaCl concentration, plant line, and whether or not AtNXHI was inserted.

34. **The correct answer is G.** From the data given in Tables 1–3, we notice that at 64 g of NaCl, B_1 and B_2 were relatively unaffected by the presence of salt, whereas B_3 and B_4 were very affected. Although B_3 did receive the AtNHXI gene along with B_1 and B_2, it is likely that the version of this gene received by B_3 was somehow inactive.

35. **The correct answer is A.** Generally speaking, as bush height increases, so too does berry mass. A positive slope occurs when one variables increases with the other. Therefore, these lines would have positive slopes.

36. **The correct answer is H.** As heat flows through the copper rod, the heated end of the rod remains at one temperature. The time at which the initially cool end of the rod reaches this temperature is given in Figure 2. This appears to occur between the 5 and 6 minute marks on the *x*-axis of the graph.

37. **The correct answer is C.** If the heat source is removed from a uniformly heated rod, the rod will immediately begin cooling to room temperature. The length of time it takes for this to occur is given by Figure 3. The rod appears to settle to room temperature between 8 and 9 minutes.

38. **The correct answer is J.** Which end of the copper rod is closest to the heat source is unlikely to change the amount of time it takes to heat the opposite end (since it seems that the rod is the same on both ends), while each of the other given features is very likely to influence this time.

39. **The correct answer is C.** According to Figure 1, the time taken for the cool end of the copper rod to reach 100° Celsius is 5.5 minutes. However, once the heat source is removed, the temperature of the room causes the rod to cool. Once the heat source is placed against the rod end again, a significant amount of heat will have left the rod, and more than 2½ minutes will be necessary for the cool end of the rod to reach 100° Celsius.

40. **The correct answer is F.** Rod length is inversely proportional to time taken to heat the rod to a uniform temperature. The longer the rod, the more mass there is to heat. Therefore, the shortest rod is likely to take the least time to heat.

» TIPS FOR THE ACT WRITING TEST

The optional ACT Writing test asks you to write a sophisticated argument within a 40-minute time limit.

Unless you've specifically rehearsed this test, you may have never written in this format before.

It's important to be familiar with the rubric that your essay readers will use to score you.

By using your planning time to the fullest, you can make sure that you adopt a strong *position*, consider *context*, *perspectives*, and *complications* in your argument, and write a *focused*, *organized*, *well-ordered* essay.

We don't have enough time in the Boot Camp to prepare you for the ACT Writing test, but if you are planning on taking the Writing test, a good place to start is the *Preparing for the ACT* booklet. In this booklet, ACT lays out exactly what it's looking for and provides a demonstration essay for each score level.

Your writing test will be scored by two trained readers. Each reader will score your essay on a scale of 1–6 in four separate domains: 1) Ideas and Analysis, 2) Development and Support, 3) Organization, and 4) Language Use and Conventions. Each domain has a total score of 2–12, and together these are calculated into your writing score, ranging from 1–36.

Your writing score does **not** affect your composite ACT score or the scores on the multiple-choice tests. However, it does affect your English Language Arts score, which is the average of your English, reading, and writing scores, also scaled from 1–36.

In the next few pages, we'll provide you with three practice writing prompts. These are for use at home, not during the Boot Camp. Only practice with these after you've studied the writing portion of *Preparing for the ACT*.

» PRACTICE ACT WRITING PROMPT #1

Time Limit: 30 Minutes

(Write your essay on separate sheets of paper.)

Communities want to keep their teenagers safe and out of trouble, and most teens want to spend their free time as they please. Sadly, it is often difficult to reconcile these conflicting desires. A state legislature is considering enacting a 10:00 p.m. curfew for all high school students, citing the success of other restrictions on teenagers—restrictions on the legal driving age keep underage drivers from behind the wheel of a vehicle and gambling laws restrict minors from betting and playing the lottery. Yet many teenagers use their evenings constructively, participating in work and social activities that may keep them away from home later than the proposed curfew. In a society that values both teens' freedom and wellbeing, how should we think about conflicts between the wellbeing of teenagers and teenagers' autonomy? How can we best balance these ideas?

Consider the following perspectives. Each statement suggests a specific way of viewing the conflict between the wellbeing of teenagers and teenagers' autonomy.

Perspective One	Perspective Two	Perspective Three
The primary goal of our society is to keep the greatest number of people safe from harm, especially minors who are the responsibility of the entire community. When safety is at stake, sacrificing the "teenage experience" is justified.	An important part of growing up is the experience teenagers have outside of an academic setting. Perhaps restrictions on teenagers' autonomy protects their safety, but it bars teens from partaking in employment and social interactions.	The wellbeing of teenagers is the obligation of parents and guardians, and the state should not impose restrictions to undermine that authority. When laws are enacted to protect teenagers, they should not restrict others' freedoms.

Essay Task

Write a cohesive, rational essay in which you evaluate several perspectives on the issue of the wellbeing of teenagers versus teenagers' autonomy. In your writing,

- be sure to: analyze and critique the perspectives provided

- develop your own perspective on the conflict

- describe the relationship between your perspective and the ones provided

Your perspective can agree fully, partially agree, or be unique to those provided, but you must support your perspective with persuasive reasoning and detailed, logical examples.

189

» PRACTICE ACT WRITING PROMPT #2

Time Limit: 30 Minutes

(Write your essay on separate sheets of paper.)

Schools struggling to balance budget constraints and pressure to offer a competitive curriculum are finding a solution in all-digital classes. Students spend one class period in the computer lab, working on a course. Instruction is given by a teacher via live video or in a pre-recorded lesson. This method allows schools to increase the number of courses offered without overburdening teachers. However, some educators argue that a class conducted only in a computer lab increases the likelihood that students will waste time on the internet, not having an instructor to directly engage them and keep them on task. All-digital classes are viewed as a sign of progressive education, but what is lost by removing a student from live interaction with a teacher and classmates? To what extent does such a course offering help a student and to what extent is the traditional classroom setting more beneficial?

Consider the following perspectives. Each statement suggests a specific way of viewing the issue of all-digital classes.

Perspective One	**Perspective Two**	**Perspective Three**
The best education should also be economical for schools. All-digital courses allow students to move at their own pace and sample courses that would otherwise be unavailable, as well as help schools save money.	Classroom instruction cultivates students' ability to reason, debate, and collaborate with others. An all-digital course removes the teacher's expertise in helping slower students and keeping distracted students on track.	Teachers are essential in a student's education. Schools need to carefully consider whether students are better helped by a live teacher or digital instruction and offer the best option to each student.

Essay Task

Write a cohesive, rational essay in which you evaluate several perspectives on the issue of the wellbeing of teenagers versus teenagers' autonomy. In your writing, be sure to:

- analyze and critique the perspectives provided

- develop your own perspective on the conflict

- describe the relationship between your perspective and the ones provided

Your perspective can agree fully, partially agree, or be unique to those provided, but you must support your perspective with persuasive reasoning and detailed, logical examples.

» PRACTICE ACT WRITING PROMPT #3

Time Limit: 30 Minutes

(Write your essay on separate sheets of paper.)

There is no doubt that the popularity of touch-screen smartphones has grown exponentially since they first appeared on the mainstream market. That prevalence has taken hold of younger generations, especially as smartphones have become more and more inexpensive. Many high schools are responding to the pervasiveness of smartphones by implementing a no-phone policy to prevent potential distractions, such as games, texting, and social media. Others view smartphones as tools to boost learning—not hinder it—with instructive calculator, dictionary, and encyclopedia apps. In a rapidly evolving society that is constantly making technological advancements, how should we think about the use of smartphones in high schools?

Consider the following perspectives. Each statement suggests a specific way of viewing the issue of smartphones in high schools.

Perspective One	Perspective Two	Perspective Three
Smartphones have no place in a learning environment because their drawbacks greatly outweigh any benefits they may have. Schools are a space reserved for learning and should be a distraction-free zone.	The value of smartphones should not be overlooked, as they could provide a means of communication during an emergency. School faculty should monitor that phones are kept out of sight during class periods.	Schools should use every possible opportunity to foster learning, especially such a device as a smartphone, which students bring with them everywhere. Students should be held accountable for practicing restraint over distractions.

Essay Task

Write a cohesive, rational essay in which you evaluate several perspectives on the issue of the wellbeing of teenagers versus teenagers' autonomy. In your writing, be sure to:

- analyze and critique the perspectives provided

- develop your own perspective on the conflict

- describe the relationship between your perspective and the ones provided

Your perspective can agree fully, partially agree, or be unique to those provided, but you must support your perspective with persuasive reasoning and detailed, logical examples.

SECTION SEVEN
Boot Camp Wrap-Up

» REMEMBER THESE KEY TEST-TAKING TECHNIQUES

- Never leave an answer blank.

- Pace yourself. You have limited time.

- Use the process of elimination.

- Trust your gut and go with what sounds right.

- Use easy questions to pick up time.

- Focus.

NOTES

_____

_____

_____

_____

_____

_____

_____

_____

_____

_____

_____

_____

_____

_____

_____

_____

» BEFORE YOUR TEST DATE

- Get enough sleep the entire week before the test.

- Eat well, especially on the days leading up to the test.

- Bring a snack with you on test day. Protein bars work great. Avoid sugar and junk food. A bottle of water is a good idea.

- If you can't do without caffeine, allow about one month before test time to minimize your intake.

- It is important to feel as well as possible both mentally and physically on the day of the exam.

- Reduce distractions! Stay away from social media for 24 hours before the test starts.

NOTES

_____

_____

_____

_____

_____

_____

_____

_____

_____

_____

_____

_____

_____

_____

_____

Official ACT® Practice

English Mini-Test #1

1 ■ ■ ■ ■ ■ ■ ■ ■ ■ 1

PASSAGE III

The Pottery of Mata Ortiz

In the early 1950s, a twelve-year-old boy named, Juan Quezada, gathered firewood
in the mountains near the village of Mata Ortiz in Chihuahua, Mexico. Though he dreamed of becoming an artist, Quezada spent all of his free time selling firewood to help support his family.

In the mountains, Quezada found shards of pots, and an occasional complete pot, painted with intricate red and black designs. These were artifacts from his ancestors, the Paquimé (or Casas Grandes) Indians, who lived in the area from about AD 1000 to AD 1400. Fascinated by the geometric designs, Quezada wondered, if he could make pots like these?

34 He dug the clay, soaked it, and tried to shape it into a pot. In time, he figured out how his ancestors had mixed the clay with volcanic ash to keep it from cracking and had used minerals found nearby to create paints. When it was time to paint his pots, Quezada designed his own complex geometric patterns.

As an adult, Quezada found a job with the railroad, but he always made time for his art. By 1976 he was selling pots to travelers and had taught several members of his family how to make pots. Three of

Quezada's pots were discovered in a junk shop in New Mexico by anthropologist Spencer MacCallum, who at first thought they were prehistoric. 36

---

31. A. NO CHANGE
B. boy named Juan Quezada
C. boy, named Juan Quezada
D. boy named Juan Quezada,

32. Which of the following alternatives to the underlined portion would NOT be acceptable?
F. pots—along with an occasional complete pot—
G. pots, along with an occasional complete pot,
H. pots, (and an occasional complete pot)
J. pots (and an occasional complete pot)

33. A. NO CHANGE
B. wondered if he could make pots like these.
C. wondered, if he could make pots like these.
D. wondered if he could make pots like these?

34. Which of the following true statements would provide the best transition from the preceding paragraph to this paragraph?
F. The village of Mata Ortiz is only three streets wide but stretches for a mile between the Casas Grandes River and the railroad tracks.
G. The patterns on Mata Ortiz pottery that Quezada admired are based on the techniques of the ancient Paquimé.
H. Quezada began working with clay from the mountains.
J. Quezada's painted designs became increasingly complex.

35. A. NO CHANGE
B. a dedication to teaching
C. a teacher of
D. has taught

36. In the preceding sentence, the clause "who at first thought they were prehistoric" primarily serves to indicate:
F. how closely Quezada had created his pots within the Paquimé tradition.
G. that Quezada's technique as a potter wasn't very well developed yet.
H. how strikingly simple Quezada's pots were in shape and design.
J. that the style of Quezada's pots was outmoded.

GO ON TO THE NEXT PAGE.

His search for their creator <u>led him</u> to Mata
₃₇

Ortiz and <u>an eventual</u> partnership with Quezada.
₃₈

MacCallum showed Quezada's pots to art dealers in the
United States, <u>the places in which</u> art galleries were soon
₃₉
offering Quezada thousands of dollars for them.

[1] Quezada helped his village with the money he
earned selling pottery, but he wanted to do <u>more so.</u> [2] So
₄₀
he taught people from Mata Ortiz to make pots. [3] Today

there are more than four hundred <u>potters around,</u> all of
₄₁

<u>which</u> make their pots by hand, following the traditions
₄₂
of the Paquimé Indians. [4] The village is thriving, and

many museums proudly display the pottery of Mata Ortiz.

[5] Each artist brought something unique to <u>they're</u>
₄₃

creations. <u>44</u>

37. **A.** NO CHANGE
    B. lead himself
    C. led himself
    D. lead him

38. Which choice most strongly suggests that Quezada's
    partnership with MacCallum was not formed right
    away upon MacCallum's arrival in Mata Ortiz?
    F. NO CHANGE
    G. a circumstantial
    H. a momentary
    J. a timely

39. **A.** NO CHANGE
    B. and it would happen there that
    C. where
    D. DELETE the underlined portion.

40. **F.** NO CHANGE
    G. more then that.
    H. more of them.
    J. more.

41. **A.** NO CHANGE
    B. people creating art now,
    C. potters in Mata Ortiz,
    D. DELETE the underlined portion and place a
    comma after the word *hundred*.

42. **F.** NO CHANGE
    G. whom
    H. them
    J. who

43. **A.** NO CHANGE
    B. his or herselves
    C. hers or his
    D. his or her

44. For the sake of the logic and coherence of this para-
    graph, Sentence 5 should be placed:
    F. where it is now.
    G. before Sentence 1.
    H. after Sentence 1.
    J. after Sentence 2.

Question 45 asks about the preceding passage
as a whole.

---

45. Suppose the writer's primary purpose had been to write
    an essay summarizing the history of pottery making in
    Mexico. Would this essay accomplish that purpose?

    A. Yes, because it discusses ancient pottery shards
    and complete pots from the Paquimé Indians and
    compares that pottery to modern designs.
    B. Yes, because it demonstrates the quality of the
    ancient pottery of the Mata Ortiz area.
    C. No, because it focuses instead on how one artist
    based his creations on ancient pottery techniques
    and shared those techniques with other artists.
    D. No, because it focuses instead on describing the
    Casas Grandes culture in ancient Mexico.

END OF ENGLISH MINI-TEST #1

» ANSWER EXPLANATIONS FOR ENGLISH MINI-TEST #1

31. The correct answer is B. Choice A is incorrect because *named Juan Quezada* is a complete thought that cannot be interrupted with a comma. Choices C and D are incorrect because one comma alone cannot come between the subject, *boy,* and the verb, *gathered.* The correct answer is B because *named Juan Quezada* is essential information, defining *which* boy. For this reason, no commas can be used around it.

32. The correct answer is H. Because the question asks which alternative is NOT acceptable, a grammatically correct answer is incorrect for this question. Choice F is incorrect because it correctly uses em dashes to set off the parenthetical phrase *along with an occasional complete pot.* Choice G is incorrect because it correctly uses commas to set off the parenthetical phrase from the rest of the sentence. Choice J is incorrect because it correctly uses parentheses to set off the parenthetical phrase. The correct answer is H: this alternative is grammatically incorrect and not acceptable, so it is the correct answer in this case. This alternative is not acceptable because commas and parentheses cannot be used together to set apart a parenthetical phrase. Only one or the other can be used.

33. The correct answer is B. Choices A and D are incorrect because this sentence is not a direct question, so a question mark cannot be used. Choice C is incorrect because *if he could make pots like these* is a dependent clause. No comma is necessary between an independent clause and the dependent clause that follows it. The correct answer is B: this sentence should end with a period since it is not a direct question, and the sentence should not have a comma between the independent and dependent clauses.

34. The correct answer is H. Choice F is incorrect because a description of the village does not provide a transition from Quezada wondering if he could create similar pots to his experimental process. Choices G and J are incorrect because although they do connect to the preceding phrase *fascinated by the geometric designs*, they do not logically connect to the sentence that follows, which describes Quezada attempting to create clay pots. The correct answer is H because the explanation that Quezada began working with clay from the mountains offers a logical transition between Quezada wondering if he could create similar pots to the process of making his own.

35. The correct answer is A. Choices B and C are incorrect because they both contain nouns rather than verbs, which create unreasonable statements: it doesn't make sense for Quezada to be *selling . . . a dedication to teaching* or *selling . . . a teacher.* Choice D is incorrect because the present perfect tense of *has taught* is not consistent with the past tense in the paragraph. The correct answer is A because the past perfect tense of *had taught* is consistent with the tense and meaning of the paragraph.

36. The correct answer is F. Choices G and J are incorrect because Quezada's *technique as a potter* not being *very well developed* and his *style* being *outmoded* are negative statements that are not consistent with Spencer MacCallum joining *an eventual partnership with Quezeda* in the next sentence. Choice H is incorrect because the designs that Quezada used are described as *intricate* and *complex*, which contradicts the statement that his pots were *strikingly simple*. The correct answer is F because the anthropologist thought that the pots were prehistoric since Quezada followed the same processes as his ancestors in creating his pottery.

37. The correct answer is A. Choices B and C are incorrect because the reflexive pronoun *himself* is used only when the subject and object of the sentence refer to the same thing, but in this sentence the subject is *search*. Choice D is incorrect because the present tense verb *lead* is inconsistent with the past tense of the passage. Because the noun *lead* sounds the same as the past tense verb *led*, this choice can be mistaken for correct. The correct answer is A because *led him* matches the past tense of the paragraph and uses the correct objective pronoun for MacCallum.

38. The correct answer is F. Choice G is incorrect because the word *circumstantial* implies that the partnership developed by chance, not that there was a delay in forming it. Choice H is incorrect because the word *momentary* implies that the partnership did not last very long, not that there was a delay in forming it. Choice J is incorrect because it indicates that the partnership had good timing but does not indicate that the partnership *was not formed right away*. The correct answer is F because *eventual* is the only option that communicates that a partnership *was not formed right away* between MacCallum and Quezada.

39. The correct answer is C. Choices A and B are incorrect because they are unnecessarily wordy and awkward. Choice D is incorrect because it creates a comma splice. The correct answer is C because *where* correctly and concisely connects *United States* to what follows.

40. The correct answer is J. Choice F is incorrect because *so* is an extraneous adverb that makes the phrasing wordier than necessary. Choice G is incorrect because it uses *then*, which is a word that indicates a time period, rather than *than*, which would be used for a comparison. Choice H is incorrect because it uses a vague pronoun, *them*, for which the antecedent is not clear. The correct answer is J because the phrase *to do more* correctly and concisely conveys the idea that Quezeda wanted his contribution to his village to be larger.

41. The correct answer is C. Choice A is incorrect because it is vague and seems to communicate that there are only four hundred potters on Earth because *around* is a very general word. Choice B is incorrect because it is also vague and makes it seem the author is claiming there are only four hundred people creating art in the world. Choice D is incorrect because we are left with the unanswered question "four hundred what?" The correct answer is C because this choice provides relevant, specific information about where the potters are located.

42. The correct answer is G. Choice F is incorrect because the pronoun *which* is not used when the antecedent is a person or persons. Choice H is incorrect because it creates a comma splice: *all of them make their pots by hand* is an independent clause that would need to be joined to the previous independent clause by a comma and a conjunction. Choice J is incorrect because *who* is the subjective form of the pronoun, but an objective pronoun is needed. The correct answer is G because the objective pronoun *whom* is correctly used as the object of the preposition *of*.

43. The correct answer is D. Choice A is incorrect because *they're* is the contraction for "they are," which does not make sense in this sentence. Choice B is incorrect because *herselves* is not a word. The reflexive pronoun "herself" can in normal contexts be only singular. Choice C is incorrect because the underlined portion of the sentence needs to be an adjective modifying the noun *creations*, but *hers* is a possessive pronoun and cannot function as such. The correct answer is D because the phrase *his or her* modifies the noun *creations* and matches the singular subject.

44. The correct answer is J. Choice F is incorrect because each artist making unique pottery does not logically follow the discussion of the village and museums. Choices G and H are incorrect because the paragraph would give a specific reference to *each artist* before the artists have been introduced. The correct answer is J because sentence 2 introduces the artists, the *people from Mata Ortiz* to whom Quezada taught pottery. It is logical to follow this with more detail about these artists.

45. The correct answer is C. Choice A is incorrect because discussing the pottery of the Paquimé Indians does not accomplish the purpose of summarizing the entire history of pottery making in Mexico. Choice B is incorrect because discussing *the quality of the ancient pottery* does not summarize the history of pottery making. Choice D is incorrect because each paragraph focuses on Quezada, not on the various aspects of the *Casas Grandes culture in ancient Mexico.* The correct answer is C because the passage focuses on Quezada, his work with pottery, and his teaching of pottery techniques to others.

English Mini-Test #2

1 ■ ■ ■ ■ ■ ■ ■ ■ 1

PASSAGE IV

Beaux Arts Architecture in the Spotlight

On West 45th Street in New York City, wedged
between buildings more than twice it's height, stands
the Lyceum Theatre. Tourists and New Yorkers

alike regularly filling this theater to its 900-seat
capacity. Most are there to attend a performance;

a few, for example, are likely to be architecture buffs

they come to admire the stunning building itself. Built in
1903, the theater exemplifies the Beaux Arts architectural
style, which fuses elements of classical Greek and Roman
design with Renaissance and Baroque details.

The Beaux Arts revival of classical Greek and Roman
architecture is apparent on first view of the theater. The
Lyceum's facade—the exterior front, or "face," of the
building—features half a dozen Corinthian columns.
Above the columns extends a horizontal stone band
called a frieze; carved into it are the classical theatrical

masks that represent comedy and tragedy. 51

46. **F.** NO CHANGE
    G. they're
    H. their
    J. its

47. **A.** NO CHANGE
    B. alike, regularly filling
    C. alike, regularly fill
    D. alike regularly fill

48. **F.** NO CHANGE
    G. consequently,
    H. however,
    J. in fact,

49. **A.** NO CHANGE
    B. there to
    C. whom
    D. they

50. **F.** NO CHANGE
    G. frieze; into which are carved
    H. frieze. Into which are carved
    J. frieze, carved into it are

51. The writer is considering adding the following
    sentence:

    > Masks figured prominently in classical Greek
    > theater performances, in part due to the fact
    > that one actor would usually play several
    > characters.

    Should the writer make this addition here?

    A. Yes, because it connects the paragraph's point
    about theatrical masks to the larger subject of clas-
    sical Greek theater.
    B. Yes, because it explains the masks' significance to
    classical Greek theater and architecture.
    C. No, because it only addresses classical Greek
    theater and doesn't include information about
    Roman theater.
    D. No, because it deviates from the paragraph's focus
    on the Lyceum Theatre's architecture.

GO ON TO THE NEXT PAGE.

Demonstrating the Beaux Arts infusion of Renaissance and Baroque details, tall, arched French windows, symmetrically placed between the columns, lighten the imposing gray limestone structure. [A] Above the windows and frieze, an exterior balcony spans the width of the gray building. [B] The balcony is fenced
52

with a balustrade, a stone railing supported by a row
53
of waist-high, vase-shaped pillars. [C] The ornate interior of the building is consistent with its elaborate exterior. [D] Not just one but two marble-finished grand staircases lead from the foyer to the midlevel seating area, called the mezzanine. Inside the theater itself, elegant chandeliers illuminate rose-colored walls
54

that have gold accents. In keeping with sumptuous
55
Beaux Arts style, curved rows of plush purple chairs

embrace the stage. 56 57

52. F. NO CHANGE
G. gray limestone
H. limestone
J. DELETE the underlined portion.

53. A. NO CHANGE
B. balustrade. Which is
C. balustrade. It being
D. balustrade, this is

54. F. NO CHANGE
G. elegantly chandelier illuminates
H. elegantly chandelier illuminate
J. elegant chandeliers illuminates

55. Which choice maintains the essay's positive tone and most strongly mimics the elaborate style of decor being described at this point in the essay?
A. NO CHANGE
B. embellished with myriad gold accents.
C. marred with gaudy accents of gold.
D. accented with gold.

56. If the writer were to delete the preceding sentence, the essay would primarily lose details that:
F. illustrate one of the Lyceum Theatre's features that deviates from Beaux Arts architecture.
G. contribute to the description of the Lyceum Theatre's elaborate interior.
H. support the essay's claim that Beaux Arts architecture was most popular in the twentieth century.
J. clarify an unfamiliar architectural term used in the essay.

57. The writer wants to divide this paragraph into two in order to separate details about the building's outdoor features from details about its indoor features. The best place to begin the new paragraph would be at Point:
A. A.
B. B.
C. C.
D. D.

GO ON TO THE NEXT PAGE.

Patrons credit the handsome Beaux Arts aesthetic
—58

with adding enhancement to their theatergoing experience.
—59
Though smaller and more cramped than many newer

theaters—audience members often note that legroom is

limited—the Lyceum's distinctive atmosphere continues

to delight theater fans as well as architecture enthusiasts.

58. F. NO CHANGE
G. In the same manner, patrons
H. On one hand, patrons
J. For instance, patrons

59. A. NO CHANGE
B. adding enhancement to the experience of
C. adding to the experience of
D. enhancing

Question 60 asks about the preceding passage as a whole.

60. Suppose the writer's primary purpose had been to explain how a building illustrates a particular architectural style. Would this essay accomplish that purpose?

F. Yes, because it describes the architectural styles of several New York theater buildings.
G. Yes, because it enumerates a number of the Lyceum Theatre's Beaux Arts features.
H. No, because it focuses more specifically on the set design for the Lyceum Theatre's productions.
J. No, because it focuses on more than one architectural style.

END OF ENGLISH MINI-TEST #2

» ANSWER EXPLANATIONS FOR ENGLISH MINI-TEST #2

46. The correct answer is J. Choice F is incorrect because *it's* is a contraction for "it is," which does not make sense in this sentence. Choice G is incorrect because *they're* is a contraction for "they are," which also does not work in this sentence. Choice H is incorrect because *their* is a plural possessive pronoun, but its antecedent, *Lyceum Theatre*, is singular. The correct answer is J because *its* is a singular possessive pronoun that agrees in number with *Lyceum Theatre*.

47. The correct answer is D. Choices A and B are incorrect because the sentence is incomplete—*filling* does not work as a verb here. Choice C is incorrect because a comma interrupts the subject and the verb. There can never be just one comma between the subject and verb. The correct answer is D because the verb *fill* makes it a complete sentence, and it does not include any unnecessary punctuation.

48. The correct answer is H. Choice F is incorrect because *architecture buffs* coming *to admire the stunning building* is not an example of most people being *there to attend a performance*. Choice G is incorrect because *architecture buffs* coming *to admire the stunning building* is not a consequence of most people being *there to attend a performance*. Choice J is incorrect because *in fact* means "actually, really, or indeed." This transition phrase indicates that the second half of the sentence further emphasizes the first half of the sentence. However, only *a few … are likely to be architecture buffs*, whereas the first half of the sentence discusses *most* people. The correct answer is H because the transition *however* indicates a contrast or contradiction. Since there is a contrast between the first and second parts of the sentence, this is the best choice.

49. The correct answer is B. Choices A and D are incorrect because they create run-on sentences by joining two independent clauses without punctuation or conjunctions. Choice C is incorrect because *whom* is the subject of the clause and should be in the subjective form, *who*, rather than the objective form, *whom*. The correct answer is B because *there to admire the stunning building itself* modifies *buffs* and avoids creating a run-on sentence.

50. The correct answer is F. Choice G is incorrect because a semicolon is supposed to join two independent clauses, but *into which are carved the classical theatrical masks that represent comedy and tragedy* is not an independent clause. Choice H is incorrect because *into which are carved …* is an incomplete sentence. Choice J is incorrect because it creates a comma splice. The correct answer is F because the semicolon shows a connection between two independent clauses. Although *carved into it are the classical theatrical masks that represent comedy and tragedy* may not appear to be an independent clause, it is simply inverted, placing the predicate before the subject (the predicate being *carved into it are* and the subject being *the classical theatrical masks*).

51. The correct answer is D. Choice A is incorrect because the paragraph does not make a point about theatrical masks but only briefly mentions them, and the main subject of the essay is the Lyceum Theatre, not *classical Greek theater*. Choice B is incorrect because this addition is not relevant to the essay, which is focused on describing the Lyceum Theater. Choice C is incorrect because even if the addition included information about Roman theater, it would not be relevant to this essay. The correct answer is D because the essay focuses on the Lyceum Theatre, and every paragraph describes some aspect of the building's architecture. It is not relevant to discuss in detail how *masks figured prominently in classical Greek theater performances*.

52. The correct answer is J. Choices F, G, and H are incorrect because *gray* and *limestone* are already mentioned in the preceding sentence. The correct answer is J because it is the only option that is not redundant.

53. The correct answer is A. Choice B is incorrect because the clause beginning with *which is a stone railing* is a dependent clause and cannot stand on its own as a complete sentence. Choice C is incorrect because the sentence is incomplete—*being supported* is a verbal phrase, not a verb. Choice D is incorrect because it forms a comma splice between the two independent clauses. The correct answer is A because it correctly uses a comma to separate the parenthetical phrase, which begins with *a stone railing*, from the noun it describes, *balustrade*.

54. The correct answer is F. Choices G and H are incorrect because the adverb *elegantly* modifies the noun *chandelier*, but it should be in the adjective form, *elegant*. Choice J is incorrect because the verb *illuminates* is singular and does not agree with the plural subject *chandeliers*. The correct answer is F because this choice correctly uses the adjective *elegant* to modify the noun *chandeliers*, and the plural verb *illuminate* agrees in number with the subject, *chandeliers*.

55. The correct answer is B. Choices A and D are incorrect because they do not involve an *elaborate style*. Choice C is incorrect because the word *marred* is negative, a synonym of "ruined" or "scarred," and so does not maintain a *positive tone*. The correct answer is B because *embellished* and *myriad* are the most elaborate word choices that still maintain a *positive tone*.

56. The correct answer is G. Choice F is incorrect because the sentence begins with *in keeping with sumptuous Beaux Arts style*, which means that the *features* do not deviate *from Beaux Arts architecture*. Choice H is incorrect because the essay does not make this claim. Choice J is incorrect because this sentence does not define or clarify any architectural terms. The correct answer is G because this paragraph describes the interior of the theater, and this sentence adds specific details about the furniture inside.

57. The correct answer is C. Choices A and B are incorrect because dividing the paragraph in either of these two positions will group details about the *exterior balcony* with details about the *indoor features* that appear later in the paragraph. Choice D is incorrect because it groups a sentence about the interior with earlier details about the building's exterior features. The correct answer is C because all of the sentences before this point discuss *outdoor features*, while all of the sentences after this point discuss *indoor features*.

58. The correct answer is F. Choice G is incorrect because *patrons* crediting an *aesthetic* is not acting *in the same manner* or way as *rows of plush purple chairs* embracing the stage. Choice H is incorrect because *on one hand* introduces a discussion about two items, but a second item is not mentioned. Choice J is incorrect because *patrons credit the handsome Beaux Arts aesthetic* is not an *instance* (example) of how *rows of plush purple chairs embrace the stage*. The correct answer is F because it is the only choice that does not include an inappropriate transition. No transitional words are needed to change topics in this paragraph.

59. The correct answer is D. Choice A is incorrect because *adding enhancement to* is wordy and unnecessary. Choices B and C are incorrect because the word *experience* is stated later in the sentence, so it is redundant to repeat it here. The correct answer is D because *enhancing* is the most concise choice, communicating the same meaning as choices A, B, and C in a single word.

60. The correct answer is G. Choice F is incorrect because the essay does not focus on any other theater buildings in New York besides the Lyceum Theatre. Choice H is incorrect because the essay does not give any details about set design. Choice J is incorrect because the essay focuses only on the Beaux Arts architectural style. The correct answer is G because in each paragraph, the passage *enumerates* the *Lyceum Theatre's Beaux Arts features*. The title of the essay, "Beaux Arts Architecture in the Spotlight," gives us a clue that the author seeks to illustrate *a particular architectural style*: Beaux Arts. The passage describes one building, the Lyceum Theatre, to accomplish this.

Math Mini-Test #1

2 △ △ △ △ △ △ △ △ △ **2**

DO YOUR FIGURING HERE

21. To get a driver's license, an applicant must pass a written test and a driving test. Past records show that 80% of the applicants pass the written test and 60% of those who have passed the written test pass the driving test. Based on these figures, how many applicants in a random group of 1,000 applicants would you expect to get driver's licenses?

    A. 200
    B. 480
    C. 600
    D. 750
    E. 800

22. If a, b, and c are positive integers such that $a^b = x$ and $c^b = y$, then $xy = $?

    F. ac^b
    G. ac^{2b}
    H. $(ac)^b$
    J. $(ac)^{2b}$
    K. $(ac)^{b^2}$

23. Which of the following expressions is equivalent to $\frac{1}{2}y^2(6x + 2y + 12x - 2y)$?

    A. $9xy^2$
    B. $18xy$
    C. $3xy^2 + 12x$
    D. $9xy^2 - 2y^3$
    E. $3xy^2 + 12x - y^3 - 2y$

24. An artist makes a profit of $(500p - p^2)$ dollars from selling p paintings. What is the fewest number of paintings the artist can sell to make a profit of at least $60,000 ?

    F. 100
    G. 150
    H. 200
    J. 300
    K. 600

25. Last month, Lucie had total expenditures of $900. The pie chart below breaks down these expenditures by category. The category in which Lucie's expenditures were greatest is what percent of her total expenditures, to the nearest 1% ?

    A. 24%
    B. 28%
    C. 32%
    D. 34%
    E. 39%

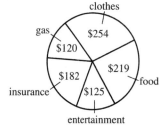

GO ON TO THE NEXT PAGE.

2 △ △ △ △ △ △ △ △ △ **2**

26. In the figure shown below, the measure of $\angle BAC$ is $(x + 20)°$ and the measure of $\angle BAD$ is $90°$. What is the measure of $\angle CAD$?

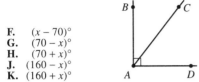

    F. $(x - 70)°$
    G. $(70 - x)°$
    H. $(70 + x)°$
    J. $(160 - x)°$
    K. $(160 + x)°$

27. What is the perimeter, in inches, of the isosceles right triangle shown below, whose hypotenuse is $8\sqrt{2}$ inches long?

    A. 8
    B. $8 + 8\sqrt{2}$
    C. $8 + 16\sqrt{2}$
    D. 16
    E. $16 + 8\sqrt{2}$

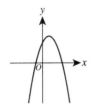

28. The equation $y = ax^2 + bx + c$ is graphed in the standard (x, y) coordinate plane below for real values of a, b, and c. When $y = 0$, which of the following best describes the solutions for x ?

    F. 2 distinct positive real solutions
    G. 2 distinct negative real solutions
    H. 1 positive real solution and 1 negative real solution
    J. 2 real solutions that are not distinct
    K. 2 distinct solutions that are not real

29. What is the product of the complex numbers $(-3i + 4)$ and $(3i + 4)$?

    A. 1
    B. 7
    C. 25
    D. $-7 + 24i$
    E. $7 + 24i$

30. The radius of the base of the right circular cone shown below is 5 inches, and the height of the cone is 7 inches. Solving which of the following equations gives the measure, θ, of the angle formed by a slant height of the cone and a radius?

    F. $\tan \theta = \frac{5}{7}$

    G. $\tan \theta = \frac{7}{5}$

    H. $\sin \theta = \frac{5}{7}$

    J. $\sin \theta = \frac{7}{5}$

    K. $\cos \theta = \frac{7}{5}$

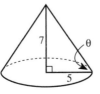

END OF MATH MINI-TEST #1

» ANSWER EXPLANATIONS FOR MATH MINI-TEST #1

21. **The correct answer is B.** In order to solve this problem, you must convert the percentages into decimals by dividing by 100. If we start with 1,000 and 80% pass the written test, then $1,000 \cdot 0.8 = 800$ students pass the written test. If, of those 800 students, 60% pass the driving test, then $800 \cdot 0.6 = 480$ students pass the driving test and get a license.

22. **The correct answer is H.** Assume that $b = 3$. Then
$xy = a^3c^3 = aaaccc = acacac = (ac)^3$. For all positive integers b, $xy = (ac)^b$.

23. **The correct answer is A.** Distribute $\frac{1}{2} y^2$ to the terms in parentheses.

$\frac{1}{2} y^2(6x + 2y + 12x - 2y) = 3xy^2 + y^3 + 6xy^2 - y^3$

Combine like terms.

$9xy^2$

24. **The correct answer is H.** Create an equation in which the given expression is set equal to $60,000 and solve for p.

$500p - p^2 = 60,000$

$p^2 - 500p + 60,000 = 0$

$(p - 200)(p - 300) = 0$

$p = 200 \text{ or } 300$

Since we are looking for the *fewest* number of paintings, 200 is the best choice.

25. **The correct answer is B.** At $254, clothes are Lucie's greatest expenditure. Divide by the total amount of expenditures, $900.

$\frac{\$254}{\$900} = 0.282$

Multiply by 100 to express as a percentage, then round to find the answer.

$0.282 = 28.2\% \approx 28\%$

26. **The correct answer is G.** $\angle BAC$ plus $\angle CAD$ must equal 90° since these two angles make up $\angle BAD$. We subtract the measure of $\angle BAC$ from 90° to find the measure of $\angle CAD$.

$90° - (x + 20)° = 90° - x° - 20° = 70° - x° = (70 - x)°$

27. The correct answer is E. The sides of an isosceles right triangle adhere to the following proportionality: $x, x, x\sqrt{2}$. Since the hypotenuse has a length of $8\sqrt{2}$, the lengths of the other two sides must each be 8. Add the sides to find the perimeter.

$$8 + 8 + 8\sqrt{} = 16 + 8\sqrt{2}$$

28. The correct answer is H. There are two points on the graph where $y = 0$. These are the points where the curve touches the x-axis. One of these points corresponds to a negative x value, the other to a positive x value. Therefore, *1 positive real solution and 1 negative real solution* is the best description for the solutions for x.

29. The correct answer is C. Use the FOIL method and combine like terms.

$$(-3i + 4)(3i + 4) = -9i^2 - 12i + 12i + 16 = -9(-1) + 16 = 25$$

30. The correct answer is G. The tangent of an angle is defined as the length of the side opposite of the angle divided by the length of the side adjacent to the angle: $\tan\theta = \dfrac{\text{opposite}}{\text{adjacent}}$. The opposite length is 7, and the adjacent length is 5, so $\tan\theta = \dfrac{7}{5}$ gives the equation that, if solved, provides the value of θ.

Math Mini-Test #2

31. To make a 750-piece jigsaw puzzle more challenging, a puzzle company includes 5 extra pieces in the box along with the 750 pieces, and those 5 extra pieces do not fit anywhere in the puzzle. If you buy such a puzzle box, break the seal on the box, and immediately select 1 piece at random, what is the probability that it will be 1 of the extra pieces?

A. $\frac{1}{5}$

B. $\frac{1}{755}$

C. $\frac{1}{750}$

D. $\frac{5}{755}$

E. $\frac{5}{750}$

32. What fraction lies exactly halfway between $\frac{2}{3}$ and $\frac{3}{4}$?

F. $\frac{3}{5}$

G. $\frac{5}{6}$

H. $\frac{7}{12}$

J. $\frac{9}{16}$

K. $\frac{17}{24}$

DO YOUR FIGURING HERE

GO ON TO THE NEXT PAGE.

2 △ △ △ △ △ △ △ △ △ **2**

Use the following information to answer questions 33–35.

Gianna is converting a 12-foot-by-15-foot room in her house to a craft room. Gianna will install tile herself but will have CC Installations build and install the cabinets. The scale drawing shown below displays the location of the cabinets in the craft room (0.25 inch represents 2 feet).

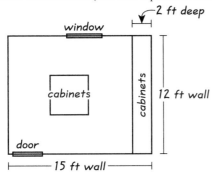

Cabinets will be installed along one of the 12-foot walls from floor to ceiling, and 4 cabinets that are each 3 feet tall will be installed in the middle of the room. These are the only cabinets that will be installed, and each of them will be 2 feet wide and 2 feet deep. CC Installations has given Gianna an estimate of $2,150.00 for building and installing the cabinets.

33. A 15-foot wall is how many inches long in the scale drawing?

   A. 1.5
   B. 1.875
   C. 3
   D. 3.375
   E. 3.75

34. Gianna will install tile on the portion of the floor that will NOT be covered by cabinets. What is the area, in square feet, of the portion of the floor that will NOT be covered by cabinets?

   F. 72
   G. 90
   H. 140
   J. 156
   K. 164

35. CC Installations' estimate consists of a $650.00 charge for labor, plus a fixed charge per cabinet. The labor charge and the charge per cabinet remain the same for any number of cabinets built and installed. CC Installations would give Gianna what estimate if the craft room were to have twice as many cabinets as Gianna is planning to have?

   A. $2,800.00
   B. $3,000.00
   C. $3,450.00
   D. $3,650.00
   E. $4,300.00

GO ON TO THE NEXT PAGE.

2 △ △ △ △ △ △ △ △ △ **2**

36. Which of the following is the graph of the region $1 < x + y < 2$ in the standard (x,y) coordinate plane?

DO YOUR FIGURING HERE

F.
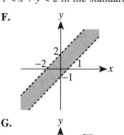

J.
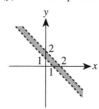

G.
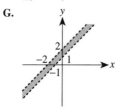

K.
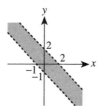

H.
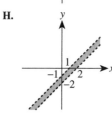

37. What is the difference between the mean and the median of the set {3, 8, 10, 15} ?
   A. 0
   B. 1
   C. 4
   D. 9
   E. 12

38. Which of the following describes a true relationship between the functions $f(x) = (x - 3)^2 + 2$ and $g(x) = \frac{1}{2}x + 1$ graphed below in the standard (x,y) coordinate plane?

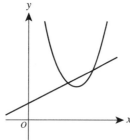

   F. $f(x) = g(x)$ for exactly 2 values of x
   G. $f(x) = g(x)$ for exactly 1 value of x
   H. $f(x) < g(x)$ for all x
   J. $f(x) > g(x)$ for all x
   K. $f(x)$ is the inverse of $g(x)$

GO ON TO THE NEXT PAGE.

2 △ △ △ △ △ △ △ △ △ **2**

Use the following information to answer
questions 39–40.

Trapezoid *ABCD* is graphed in the standard (*x,y*) coordinate
plane below.

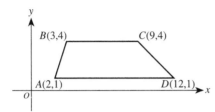

39. What is the slope of $\overline{CD}$?

   A. −3

   B. −1

   C. 1

   D. $\frac{5}{21}$

   E. $\frac{3}{2}$

40. When *ABCD* is reflected over the *y*-axis to *A′B′C′D′*,
what are the coordinates of *D′* ?

   F. (−12, 1)
   G. (−12, −1)
   H. (12, −1)
   J. (1, 12)
   K. (1,−12)

END OF MATH MINI-TEST #2

» ANSWER EXPLANATIONS FOR MATH MINI-TEST #2

31. The correct answer is D. To find the probability, determine the number of desired outcomes and divide by the number of possible outcomes. There are 5 desired outcomes (extra pieces) and $750 + 5 = 755$ possible outcomes, so the probability of selecting one of the extra pieces is $\dfrac{5}{755}$.

32. The correct answer is K. Convert the two fractions so they share a common denominator. $\dfrac{2}{3} = \dfrac{8}{12}$ and $\dfrac{3}{4} = \dfrac{9}{12}$. The numerator between 8 and 9 is 8.5, which is not an available answer choice, so convert the fractions to sharing denominators of 24. $\dfrac{8}{12} = \dfrac{16}{24}$ and $\dfrac{9}{12} = \dfrac{18}{24}$. Now it is clear that the number between the numerators is 17, so the fraction that lies exactly halfway between $\dfrac{2}{3}$ and $\dfrac{3}{4}$ is $\dfrac{17}{24}$.

33. The correct answer is B. The first paragraph of the text states that *0.25 inch represents 2 feet*. Set up and solve a proportion to determine the length of the wall in the scale drawing.

$$\dfrac{0.25}{2} = \dfrac{x}{15}$$

$$2x = 3.75$$

$$x = 1.875$$

34. The correct answer is H. Find the area of the room.

$$15 \cdot 12 = 180$$

Subtract the area covered by the cabinets. The four middle cabinets are each 2 by 2, so their total area is $4(2 \cdot 2)$.

$$180 - (12 \cdot 2) - 4(2 \cdot 2) = 180 - 24 - 16 = 140$$

35. The correct answer is D. Find the charge per cabinet. First subtract the labor charge from the total charge then divide by the total number of cabinets. There were 4 cabinets in the middle and, since each cabinet is 2 feet wide, $12 \div 2 = 6$ cabinets along the side of the wall: 10 cabinets total.

$$\$2,150 - \$650 = \$1,500$$

$$\dfrac{\$1,500}{10} = \$150$$

Each cabinet costs $150. If there were twice as many cabinets, $10 \cdot 2 = 20$, then there would be the $650 labor cost plus $20 \cdot \$150 = \$3,000$ for the cabinets for a total charge of $\$650 + \$3,000 = \$3,650$.

36. The correct answer is J. The inequality $1 < x + y < 2$ is actually two inequalities: $1 < x + y$ and $x + y < 2$. Convert both of these to slope-intercept form so that you can visualize the lines (or graph them on your calculator).

$1 < x + y$

$y > -x + 1$

and

$x + y < 2$

$y < -x + 2$

So, we are looking for two lines with a slope of -1 and y-intercepts of 1 and 2. The only two graphs that have y-intercepts of 1 and 2 are choices G and J. Between choices G and J, only choice J has lines with negative slopes.

37. The correct answer is A. To find the mean of the data set, add the terms then divide by the number of terms.

$$\frac{3+8+10+15}{4} = \frac{36}{4} = 9$$

To find the median, sort the terms then take the middle term. Since two terms, 8 and 10, make up the middle, find their average.

$$\frac{8+10}{2} = \frac{18}{2} = 9$$

Subtract the median from the mean to find the difference.

$$9 - 9 = 0$$

38. The correct answer is F. Since $g(x)$ intersects with $f(x)$ at exactly two distinct points on the graph, $f(x) = g(x)$ for exactly two values of x.

39. The correct answer is B. The slope formula is $\frac{y_2 - y_1}{x_2 - x_1}$. Insert the coordinates for C and D into the formula to determine the slope.

$$\frac{1-4}{12-9} = \frac{-3}{3} = -1$$

40. The correct answer is F. Since point D is being reflected across the y-axis, its x-coordinate will become negative while its y-coordinate remains the same. Therefore, the coordinates of D' are $(-12, 1)$.

Reading Mini-Test #1

Passage III

HUMANITIES: Passage A is adapted from the essay "Just This Side of Byzantium" by Ray Bradbury (©1975 by Ray Bradbury), which is the introduction to a later edition of Bradbury's 1957 novel *Dandelion Wine*. Passage B is adapted from *Dandelion Wine* (©1957 by Ray Bradbury).

Passage A by Ray Bradbury

I began to learn the nature of surprises, thankfully, when I was fairly young as a writer. Before that, like every beginner, I thought you could beat, pummel, and thrash an idea into existence. Under such treatment, of
5 course, any decent idea folds up its paws, turns on its back, fixes its eyes on eternity, and dies.

It was with great relief, then, that in my early twenties I floundered into a word-association process in which I simply got out of bed each morning, walked to
10 my desk, and put down any word or series of words that happened along in my head.

I would then take arms against the word, or for it, and bring on an assortment of characters to weigh the word and show me its meaning in my own life. An hour
15 or two hours later, to my amazement, a new story would be finished and done. The surprise was total and lovely. I soon found that I would have to work this way for the rest of my life.

First I rummaged my mind for words that could
20 describe my personal nightmares, fears of night and time from my childhood, and shaped stories from these.

Then I took a long look at the green apple trees and the old house I was born in and the house next door where lived my grandparents, and all the lawns of the
25 summers I grew up in, and I began to try words for all that.

I had to send myself back, with words as catalysts, to open the memories out and see what they had to offer.

30 So from the age of twenty-four to thirty-six hardly a day passed when I didn't stroll myself across a recollection of my grandparents' northern Illinois grass, hoping to come across some old half-burnt firecracker, a rusted toy, or a fragment of letter written to myself in
35 some young year hoping to contact the older person I became to remind him of his past, his life, his people, his joys, and his drenching sorrows.

Along the way I came upon and collided, through word-association, with old and true friendships. I bor-
40 rowed my friend John Huff from my childhood in Arizona and shipped him East to Green Town so that I could say good-bye to him properly.

Along the way, I sat me down to breakfasts, lunches, and dinners with the long dead and much
45 loved.

Thus I fell into surprise. I came on the old and best ways of writing through ignorance and experiment and was startled when truths leaped out of bushes like quail before gunshot. I blundered into creativity as any child
50 learning to walk and see. I learned to let my senses and my Past tell me all that was somehow true.

Passage B by Ray Bradbury

The facts about John Huff, aged twelve, are simple and soon stated. He could pathfind more trails than anyone since time began, could leap from the sky like a
55 chimpanzee from a vine, could live underwater two minutes and slide fifty yards downstream from where you last saw him. The baseballs you pitched him he hit in the apple trees, knocking down harvests. He ran laughing. He sat easy. He was not a bully. He was kind.
60 He knew the names of all the wild flowers and when the moon would rise and set. He was, in fact, the only god living in the whole of Green Town, Illinois, during the twentieth century that Douglas Spaulding knew of.

And right now he and Douglas were hiking out
65 beyond town on another warm and marble-round day, the sky blue blown-glass reaching high, the creeks bright with mirror waters fanning over white stones. It was a day as perfect as the flame of a candle.

Douglas walked through it thinking it would go on
70 this way forever. The sound of a good friend whistling like an oriole, pegging the softball, as you horse-danced, key-jingled the dusty paths; things were at hand and would remain.

It was such a fine day and then suddenly a cloud
75 crossed the sky, covered the sun, and did not move again.

John Huff had been speaking quietly for several minutes. Now Douglas stopped on the path and looked over at him.

80 "John, say that again."

"You heard me the first time, Doug."

"Did you say you were—going away?"

John took a yellow and green train ticket solemnly from his pocket and they both looked at it.

85 "Tonight!" said Douglas. "My gosh! Tonight we were going to play Red Light, Green Light and Statues! How come, all of a sudden? You been here in Green Town all my life. You just don't pick up and leave!"

"It's my father," said John. "He's got a job in Mil-
90 waukee. We weren't sure until today . . . "

They sat under an old oak tree on the side of the hill looking back at town. Out beyond, in sunlight, the town was painted with heat, the windows all gaping. Douglas wanted to run back in there where the town, by
95 its very weight, its houses, their bulk, might enclose and prevent John's ever getting up and running off.

GO ON TO THE NEXT PAGE.

3 ▬▬▬▬▬▬▬▬▬▬▬▬▬▬▬▬▬▬▬▬ 3

Questions 21–25 ask about Passage A.

21. When Bradbury claims, "Thus I fell into surprise" (line 46), he's most nearly referring to the:

   A. discovery that for him the secret to a creative outpouring was to use a word-association method to write fiction.
   B. long-forgotten experiences he would remember when he would talk with his childhood friends in person.
   C. realization that he wrote more effectively about his current experiences than about his past.
   D. several methods other writers taught him to help him write honest, authentic stories.

22. Passage A indicates that Bradbury believes all beginning writers think that they can:

   F. learn the nature of surprises.
   G. force an idea into creation.
   H. use one word as a catalyst for a story.
   J. become a good writer through experiment.

23. Bradbury's claim "I would then take arms against the word, or for it" (line 12) most strongly suggests that during his writing sessions, Bradbury would:

   A. attempt to find the one word that for him was the key to understanding John Huff.
   B. often reject a word as not being a catalyst for meaningful writing.
   C. deliberately choose to write only about a word that inspired his fears.
   D. feel as though he were struggling to find a word's significance to him.

24. In the seventh paragraph of Passage A (lines 30–37), Bradbury explains his habit, over many years as a writer, of almost daily:

   F. looking at and writing about objects from his childhood that he had saved.
   G. wishing he had kept more letters from his childhood to trigger his memories.
   H. driving past his grandparents' property, hoping to notice something that would remind him of his past.
   J. thinking about his grandparents' property, hoping to remember something that would bring his past into focus.

25. Passage A explains that when writing about the character John Huff, Bradbury had:

   A. placed John in a town in Arizona, where Bradbury himself had grown up.
   B. included John in stories about a town in Arizona and in stories about Green Town.
   C. "moved" John to a town other than the town in which the real-life John Huff had grown up.
   D. "borrowed" John to use as a minor character in many of his stories.

Questions 26 and 27 ask about Passage B.

26. In the first paragraph of Passage B (lines 52–63), the narrator describes John Huff in a manner that:

   F. emphasizes John's physical strength and intelligence, to indicate John's view of himself.
   G. exaggerates John's characteristics and actions, to reflect Douglas's idolization of John.
   H. highlights John's reckless behavior, to show that Douglas was most fond of John's rebelliousness.
   J. showcases John's talents, to make clear why both children and adults admired John.

27. Within Passage B, the image in lines 74–76 functions figuratively to suggest that:

   A. John's leaving on a stormy night was fitting, given Douglas's sadness.
   B. John's disappointment about moving was reflected in his mood all day.
   C. the mood of the day changed dramatically and irreversibly once John shared his news.
   D. the sky in Green Town became cloudy at the moment John told Douglas he was moving.

Questions 28–30 ask about both passages.

28. Both Passage A and Passage B highlight Bradbury's use of:

   F. a first person omniscient narrator to tell a story.
   G. satire and irony to develop characters.
   H. allegory to present a complex philosophical question.
   J. sensory details and imaginative description to convey ideas.

29. Based on Bradbury's description in Passage A of his writing process, which of the following methods hypothetically depicts a way Bradbury might have begun to write the story in Passage B?

   A. Taking notes while interviewing old friends after first deciding to write a story about two boys
   B. Forming two characters, determining that he would like to tell a story about loss, and then beginning to write a scene
   C. Writing down the words *train ticket* and then spending an hour writing whatever those words brought to his mind
   D. Outlining the plot of a story about two boys that would end with one boy leaving on a train

---

GO ON TO THE NEXT PAGE.

30. Elsewhere in the essay from which Passage A is adapted, Bradbury writes:

> Was there a real boy named John Huff?
>
> There was. And that was truly his name. But he didn't go away from me, I went away from him.

How do these statements apply to both the information about Bradbury's approach as a storyteller provided in Passage A and the story of John Huff provided in Passage B?

F. They reveal that Bradbury believed that to surprise readers is a fiction writer's most important task.

G. They reinforce that Bradbury used his life experiences to create fiction but also altered those experiences as he pleased.

H. They prove that Bradbury felt such pain over leaving John that he had to reverse events to be able to write the story.

J. They indicate that Bradbury rarely used his life experiences to create fiction.

END OF READING MINI-TEST #1

» ANSWER EXPLANATIONS FOR READING MINI-TEST #1

21. **The correct answer is A.** Choice B is incorrect because the narrator is using his memory, sending himself back *to open the memories out and see what they had to offer* (lines 28–29). He is not meeting with old acquaintances in person. Choice C is incorrect because lines 38–45 clearly refer to the narrator's past, not his current experiences. Choice D is incorrect because the narrator *came on the old and best ways of writing through ignorance and experiment* (lines 46–47), not through methods that other writers taught him. The correct answer is A because the word *thus* on line 46 means "in this way" and summarizes the many paragraphs that came before it. The main topic of Passage A is about how the narrator *floundered into a word-association process* (line 8) and its beneficial effect on his craft.

22. **The correct answer is G.** Choices F, H, and J are incorrect because the narrator mentions beginning writers only in the first paragraph, and in this context, he does not discuss learning the nature of surprises, using one word as a catalyst for a story, or experimenting one's way to being a good writer. The correct answer is G because the narrator states in lines 2–4 that *like every beginner, I thought you could beat, pummel, and thrash an idea into existence.* This is similar to the idea of forcing *an idea into creation*.

23. **The correct answer is D.** Choice A is incorrect because Bradbury's writing sessions were not only about understanding John Huff. In lines 44–45, he states that his writing let him sit down *with the long dead and much loved*, which is plural. Choices B and C are incorrect because there is no support in the passage for the idea that the narrator either rejected a word during his writing sessions or selected only words that inspired his fears. The correct answer is D because lines 13–14 make it clear that the narrator did this to *bring on an assortment of characters to weigh the word and show me its meaning in my own life*. This information supports the concept of the narrator's struggling to find the significance of a particular word.

24. **The correct answer is J.** Choices F, G, and H are incorrect because they all involve physically looking at objects from the narrator's past, but the seventh paragraph concerns the narrator's memories, indicated by the word *recollection*. The correct answer is J because lines 30–32 state that *hardly a day passed when I didn't stroll myself across a recollection of my grandparents' northern Illinois grass.* The narrator then goes on to describe how he tries to remember objects from his childhood there. This evidence closely supports choice J.

25. **The correct answer is C.** Choice A is incorrect because in one story, the narrator placed John away from Arizona, in Green Town (lines 40–41). Choices B and D are incorrect because there is no evidence in the passage that the narrator used John in multiple stories, either in Arizona or as a minor character. The correct answer is C because lines 39–41 say that the narrator *borrowed* John *and shipped him East to Green Town*. This closely supports the concept that the narrator "moved" John to a town other than the one *in which the real-life John Huff had grown up*.

26. The correct answer is G. Choice F is incorrect because the phrase *that Douglas Spaulding knew of* (line 63) indicates that this paragraph is from the point of view of Douglas, not John Huff. Choice H is incorrect because although the paragraph does include some details about John Huff that might lead you to characterize him as *reckless*, there is not much support for his being rebellious or for the narrator's being *most fond* of that aspect of John's character. Choice J is incorrect because there is no mention in this paragraph of how children and adults admire John. The correct answer is G because Douglas considers John to be *the only god living in the whole of Green Town* (lines 61–62), which is best expressed as *idolization*. The descriptions of John are also exaggerations; this paragraph uses hyperbole to give a glimpse of how Douglas viewed John.

27. The correct answer is C. Choice A is incorrect because the image of a cloud covering the sun does not provide supporting evidence that there would be a stormy night. Choice B is incorrect because line 74 says it had been *such a fine day*, so it is inaccurate to say that John's disappointment *was reflected in his mood all day*. Choice D is incorrect because the question asks how the image *functions figuratively*, but this answer choice describes what occurred literally. The correct answer is C because the image on lines 74–76 describes a dramatic and permanent change from a *fine day* to a cloudy one. This supports the expression that the mood of the day was changed dramatically and irreversibly after John said he was moving.

28. The correct answer is J. Choice F is incorrect because *first person omniscient* narration would provide insight into the thoughts of other characters besides the narrator, but there is no supporting evidence for this in the passages. Choice G is incorrect because there is little supporting evidence of *satire* or *irony* in either passage. *Satire* is a type of criticism that makes heavy use of humor. *Irony* occurs when the reader sees the meaning or consequences of a character's thoughts, statements, and actions in a way the character does not realize. Choice H is incorrect because neither passage poses a complex philosophical question. Furthermore, an *allegory* is a work that usually uses its parts, such as characters, to represent a deeper moral, political, or philosophical meaning, which is not present in these passages. The correct answer is J because both passages lean heavily on *sensory details* and *imaginative description*, such as *any decent idea folds up its paws, turns on its back, fixes its eyes on eternity, and dies* (lines 5–6) and *could leap from the sky like a chimpanzee from a vine* (lines 54–55). *Sensory details* are descriptions of sights, sounds, touches, tastes, and smells used to make writing more interesting to the reader.

29. The correct answer is C. Choices A, B, and D are incorrect because *taking notes*, *forming . . . characters*, and *outlining the plot* are three writing techniques that do not conform with the writing process that Bradbury described in Passage A. The correct answer is C because Passage A details a *word-association process* (line 8) that Bradbury used *from the age of twenty-four to thirty-six* (line 30), during which time he came up with a story that involved John Huff, one of the central characters in Passage B. Choice C describes what may have occurred in the word-association process that became the basis of Passage B.

30. The correct answer is G. Choice F is incorrect because the lines given in the question do not concern *surprise*. Choice H is incorrect because there is no support in the passage or lines provided in the question for the idea that *Bradbury felt such pain* or the concept that reversing *events* would somehow relieve that pain. Choice J is incorrect because the fact that there really was a John Huff directly contradicts the claim that *Bradbury rarely used his life experiences to create fiction*. The correct answer is G because the quote in the question supports the claim that Bradbury used his life experiences in his writing because John Huff really existed. It also supports the claim that Bradbury would alter his experiences in the writing process because he switches which childhood friend moves away from the other.

Reading Mini-Test #2

3 ━━━━━━━━━━━━━━━━━━━━━━━━━━━━━━━━━ **3**

Passage IV

NATURAL SCIENCE: This passage is adapted from the article "The Jaws That Jump" by Adam Summers (©2006 by Natural History Magazine, Inc.).

Recently I was reminded of just how powerful ants can be when inflicting damage on intruders. A team of biomechanists has studied the incredibly speedy bite of a group of Central and South American ants. The team
5 clocked the bite as the fastest on the planet—and discovered that it also gives the ants the unique ability to jump with their jaws, adding to an impressive array of already known defenses.

Trap-jaw ants nest in leaf litter, rather than under-
10 ground or in mounds. There they often feed on well-armored and elusive prey, including other species of ants. As they stalk their dinner, the trap-jaws hold their mandibles wide apart, often cocked open at 180 degrees or more by a latch mechanism. When minute trigger
15 hairs on the inner edge of the mandible come in contact with something, the jaws snap shut at speeds now known to reach 145 miles per hour. No passerby could outrace that. The astoundingly high speed gives the jaws, despite their light weight, enough force to crack
20 open the armor of most prey and get at the tasty meat inside.

The key to the jaws' speed (and their even more amazing acceleration) is that the release comes from stored energy produced by the strong but slow muscles
25 of the jaw. Think how an archer slowly draws an arrow in a bowstring against the flex of a bow: nearly all the energy from the archer's muscles pours into the flexing of the bow. When released, the energy stored in the bow wings the arrow toward its target much faster than the
30 archer could by throwing the arrow like a javelin. The biomechanics of energy storage is the domain of Sheila N. Patek and Joseph E. Baio, both biomechanists at the University of California, Berkeley. They teamed up with two ant experts, Brian L. Fisher of the California
35 Academy of Sciences in San Francisco and Andrew V. Suarez of the University of Illinois at Urbana-Champaign, to look at the trap-jaw ant *Odontomachus bauri*.

Fisher, Suarez, and other field biologists had
40 already noted that catching *O. bauri* was like grabbing for popping popcorn—and very hot popcorn at that, because a painful sting goes with an ant's trap-jaw bite. The insects bounced around in a dizzying frenzy and propelled themselves many times their body length
45 when biologists or smaller intruders approached them. Patek and Baio made high-speed video images of their movements, and discovered that the secret of their self-propulsion was the well-executed "firing" of their mandibles. They also observed that mandibles started to
50 decelerate before they meet—possibly to avoid self-inflicted damage. Most important, the ants had two distinct modes of aerial locomotion.

In the so-called escape jump, an ant orients its head and jaws perpendicular to the ground, then slams
55 its face straight down. That triggers the cocked mandibles to release with a force 400 times the ant's body weight, launching the insect ten or more body lengths nearly straight into the air. The ant doesn't seem to go in any particular direction, but the jump is
60 presumably fast and unpredictable enough to help the insect evade, say, the probing tongue of a lizard. Not only can the jumping ant gain height and sow confusion, but it may also get to a new vantage point from which to relaunch an attack.

65 The second kind of jaw-propelled locomotion is even more common than escape jumping. If an intruder enters the ants' nest, one of the ants bangs its jaws against the intruder, which triggers the trap-jaw and propels the interloper (if small enough) in one direc-
70 tion, out of the nest, and the ant in the other. Often the force sends the ant skimming an inch off the ground for nearly a foot. The attack, for obvious reasons, is known as the "bouncer defense." In the wild, gangs of defending ants team up to attack hostile strangers, sending
75 them head over heels out of the nest.

From an evolutionary point of view, the trap-jaws are an intriguing story. The ants clearly evolved an entirely new function, propulsion, for a system that was already useful—chewing up prey. Several lineages of
80 trap-jaw ants have independently hit on the tactic of storing energy in their jaws to penetrate well-defended prey. In *Odontomachus*, the horizontal, bouncer-defense jump could have arisen out of attempts to bite intruders, but the high, escape jump—with jaws aimed
85 directly at the ground—must have arisen from a different, perhaps accidental kind of behavior. Such a serendipitous event would have been a rare instance in which banging one's head against the ground got good results.

GO ON TO THE NEXT PAGE.

3 ━━━━━━━━━━━━━━━━━━━━━━━━━━━━━━━━━━ **3**

31. The primary purpose of the passage is to:

    A. provide an overview of the mechanics and key operations of the jaws of trap-jaw ants.
    B. analyze Patek and Baio's techniques for filming two defensive maneuvers of trap-jaw ants.
    C. compare the jaws of *Odontomachus bauri* to the jaws of other species of ants.
    D. describe the evolution of the ability of trap-jaw ants to perform an escape jump.

32. The sentence in lines 73–75 and the last sentence of the passage are examples of the author's rhetorical technique of:

    F. weaving sarcasm into a mostly casual and playful article.
    G. interjecting a lighthearted tone into a primarily technical article.
    H. integrating a slightly combative tone into an article that mostly praises two scientists' work.
    J. incorporating personal anecdotes into an article that mostly reports data.

33. As it is used in lines 81–82, the phrase *well-defended prey* most nearly refers to prey that:

    A. have a hard outer shell.
    B. attack with a lethal bite.
    C. travel and attack in groups.
    D. move quickly.

34. The passage makes clear that the main source of the speed of the jaws of the trap-jaw ant is the:

    F. ease of movement of the hinge of the jaw.
    G. continuous, steady firing of the jaw's mandibles.
    H. light weight of the jaw in relation to the ant's body weight.
    J. release of energy stored by muscles of the jaw.

35. The author uses the analogy of trying to grab popcorn as it pops in order to describe the trap-jaw ants' ability to:

    A. generate heat with their jaw movements.
    B. move to high ground in order to attack prey.
    C. attack intruders by tossing them out of the nest.
    D. bounce around frantically when intruders approach.

36. One main purpose of the last paragraph is to suggest that unlike their bouncer-defense jump, the trap-jaw ants' escape jump may have arisen through:

    F. the ants' trying and failing to bite intruders.
    G. a change in the structure of the mandibles of several lineages of ants.
    H. an accidental behavior of the ants.
    J. the ants' experiencing a positive outcome when they would attack in a large group.

37. As it is used in line 31, the word *domain* most nearly means:

    A. living space.
    B. area of expertise.
    C. taxonomic category.
    D. local jurisdiction.

38. The passage points to which of the following as a characteristic of trap-jaw ants' mandibles that prevents the ants from harming themselves with their powerful bite?

    F. A hinge prevents the mandibles from snapping together forcefully.
    G. Mandibles with cushioned inner edges provide a buffer when the mandibles snap shut.
    H. A latch mechanism prevents the mandibles from closing completely.
    J. The mandibles begin to decelerate before they meet.

39. As described in the passage, one benefit of the trap-jaw ant's escape jump is that it allows an ant to:

    A. land in position to launch a new attack on a predator.
    B. confuse a predator with a quick, sudden sting.
    C. signal to other ants using a predictable movement.
    D. point itself in whichever direction it chooses to escape.

40. When a trap-jaw ant uses the bouncer-defense jump effectively on an intruder, which creature(s), if any, will be propelled either out of the nest or in another direction?

    F. The intruder only
    G. The attacking ant only
    H. The attacking ant and the intruder
    J. Neither the attacking ant nor the intruder

END OF READING MINI-TEST #2

31. The correct answer is A. Choice B is incorrect because the passage mentions Patek and Baio filming the ants' defensive maneuvers only in lines 46–47, so analyzing filming techniques cannot be the primary purpose of the passage. Choice C is incorrect because this passage describes the jaws of *Odontomachus bauri* but does not compare them to the jaws of other ant species. Choice D is incorrect because although the last paragraph speculates about the evolution of the escape jump, this is not the primary purpose of the entire passage. The correct answer is A because the passage as a whole provides an overview of how the jaws in trap-jaw ants operate. The first paragraph introduces trap-jaw ants and their *unique ability to jump with their jaws* (lines 6–7), and the last paragraph speculates about how this function evolved.

32. The correct answer is G. Choice F is incorrect because lines 73–75 and lines 86–89 do not contain sarcasm. Furthermore, this passage is mostly technical, not casual or playful. Choice H is incorrect because lines 73–75 and 86–89 are not *combative,* which means "aggressive, argumentative." Choice J is incorrect because these lines do not give personal anecdotes. *Personal anecdotes* would be short and entertaining stories involving the narrator. The correct answer is G because the last sentence of the passage is lighthearted, joking about *banging one's head against the ground*, and lines 73–75 do present a somewhat amusing image of intruders being propelled *head over heels* from the ants' habitat.

33. The correct answer is A. Choices B, C, and D are incorrect because the context of the phrase in question explains that trap-jaw ants store *energy in their jaws to penetrate well-defended prey* (lines 80–82). The verb *penetrate* means "to force through," which would not apply to prey that attack with lethal bites, travel in groups, or move quickly. The correct answer is A because it is logical that the ants' jaws can *penetrate* prey with hard outer shells.

34. The correct answer is J. Choices F and G are incorrect because there is no support in the passage for the idea that the jaw's speed comes from easily moving the jaw hinge or steadily firing the jaw's mandibles. Choice H is incorrect because although line 19 does say the jaws are *light weight*, this characteristic is not associated with its speed. The correct answer is J because lines 22–25 explain that the speed of the jaws *comes from stored energy produced by the strong but slow muscles of the jaw.*

35. The correct answer is D. Choice A is incorrect because the author's mention of *hot popcorn* in line 41 is figurative, not literal. The ants are not actually becoming hot. Choice B is incorrect because although the passage does describe how the ants can jump to *a new vantage point from which to relaunch an attack* (lines 63–64), this is not necessarily analogous to grabbing popcorn as it pops. Choice C is incorrect because the passage's reference to throwing intruders out of their nest in lines 74–75 is not connected to the analogy of *grabbing for popping popcorn* in lines 40–41. The correct answer is D because *the insects bounced around in a dizzying frenzy . . . when biologists or smaller intruders approached them* (lines 43–45) closely matches the claim presented by choice D. Furthermore, this choice includes wording, *bounce around*, most analogous to popcorn as it pops.

36. The correct answer is H. Choice F is incorrect because the paragraph states in lines 82–84 that what evolved out of trap-jaw ants' attempts to bite intruders was the *bouncer-defense jump*, not the escape jump. Choices G and J are incorrect because the paragraph does not support the concept that the escape jump came about because of a change in mandible structure or because of positive outcomes in group attacks. The correct answer is H because the passage states in lines 84–86 that the escape jump *must have arisen from a different, perhaps accidental kind of behavior*, which is best expressed by this choice.

37. The correct answer is B. Choice A is incorrect because it does not make sense to say that the *biomechanics of energy storage* are a *living space* for scientists. Choice C is incorrect because it would designate scientists to a *taxonomic category* (a classification of organisms) called *biomechanics of energy storage*. This is illogical because scientists are humans, not biomechanics. Choice D is incorrect because a science subject cannot have a *local jurisdiction*. The correct answer is B because it is logical to assume that *the biomechanics of energy storage* would be an *area of expertise* for two *biomechanists* (lines 30–32). *Expertise* means "highly developed skill and knowledge."

38. The correct answer is J. Choices F, G, and H are incorrect because their claims are not supported by the passage. There is no evidence of hinges preventing *mandibles from snapping together*, *mandibles with cushioned inner edges*, or latch mechanisms preventing *the mandibles from closing completely*. The correct answer is J because this choice is supported by lines 49–51: *they also observed that mandibles started to decelerate before they meet—possibly to avoid self-inflicted damage.*

39. The correct answer is A. Choice B is incorrect because the escape jump described in lines 53–55 involves the ant releasing its jaws into the ground, not into a predator. Choice C is incorrect because this maneuver is described as *unpredictable* (line 60). Choice D is incorrect because with the escape jump, *the ant doesn't seem to go in any particular direction* (lines 58–59), which contradicts the claim that the ant points itself in a determined direction. The correct answer is A because this answer choice paraphrases lines 63–64, which state that the escape jump can give trap-jaw ants *a new vantage point from which to relaunch an attack.*

40. The correct answer is H. Choices F, G, and J are incorrect because they contradict the description of the bouncer defense detailed in lines 67–70. The correct answer is H because it matches the description of the bouncer defense in lines 67–70: *one of the ants bangs its jaws against the intruder, which triggers the trap-jaw and propels the interloper . . . in one direction, out of the nest, and the ant in the other.*

Science Mini-Test #1

Passage III

Greenhouse gases such as methane (CH_4) warm Earth's climate. Figure 1 shows the concentration of CH_4 in Earth's atmosphere and the solar radiation intensity at Earth's surface for tropical Europe and Asia over the past 250,000 years. As the figure shows, the CH_4 concentration and the solar radiation intensity have increased and decreased at the same times over most of this period. Figure 2 shows the same types of data for the same region over the past 11,000 years. This figure is consistent with the hypothesis that the greenhouse gases from human activities may have begun warming Earth's climate thousands of years earlier than once thought.

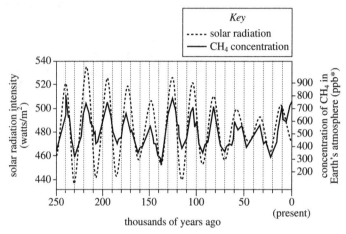

*ppb = parts per billion

Figure 1

GO ON TO THE NEXT PAGE.

4 ○ ○ ○ ○ ○ ○ ○ ○ ○ **4**

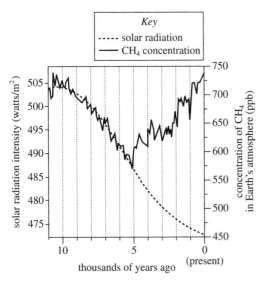

Figure 2

Figures adapted from William Ruddiman, *Plows, Plagues & Petroleum.* ©2005 by Princeton University Press.

17. Suppose that whenever the CH_4 concentration increases, a corresponding, immediate increase in average global temperature occurs, and that whenever the CH_4 concentration decreases, a corresponding, immediate decrease in average global temperature occurs. Based on Figure 2, which of the following graphs best represents a plot of average global temperature over the past 11,000 years?

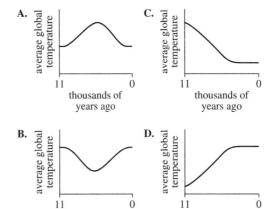

18. Based on Figure 1, the average solar radiation intensity over the past 250,000 years was closest to which of the following?

    F. 400 watts/m^2
    G. 440 watts/m^2
    H. 480 watts/m^2
    J. 520 watts/m^2

19. One *solar radiation cycle* is the time between a maximum in the solar radiation intensity and the next maximum in the solar radiation intensity. According to Figure 1, the average length of a solar radiation cycle during the past 250,000 years was:

    A. less than 15,000 years.
    B. between 15,000 years and 35,000 years.
    C. between 35,000 years and 55,000 years.
    D. greater than 55,000 years.

20. Which of the following statements best describes the primary effect of CH_4 on Earth's climate?

    F. CH_4 gives off visible light to space, cooling Earth's climate.
    G. CH_4 gives off ultraviolet radiation to space, warming Earth's climate.
    H. CH_4 absorbs heat as it enters Earth's atmosphere from space, cooling Earth's climate.
    J. CH_4 absorbs heat that comes up from Earth's surface, warming Earth's climate.

15. According to Figure 2, the solar radiation intensity 8,000 years ago was closest to which of the following?

    A. 490 watts/m^2
    B. 495 watts/m^2
    C. 500 watts/m^2
    D. 505 watts/m^2

16. According to Figure 2, if the trend in the CH_4 concentration had continued to match the trend in the solar radiation intensity, the CH_4 concentration at present would most likely be:

    F. less than 550 ppb.
    G. between 550 ppb and 600 ppb.
    H. between 600 ppb and 650 ppb.
    J. greater than 650 ppb.

END OF SCIENCE MINI-TEST #1

» ANSWER EXPLANATIONS FOR SCIENCE MINI-TEST #1

15. The correct answer is C. Choices A and B are incorrect because according to Figure 2, 490 and 495 watts/m² correspond to 6,000 and 7,000 years ago, respectively. Choice D is incorrect because 505 watts/m² corresponds to 9,000 to 10,000 years ago on Figure 2. The correct answer is C because in Figure 2, the x-axis represents *thousands of years ago*. The mark for 8,000 years ago is two marks to the right of 10 on the x-axis. The dotted line above that mark intersects with the dotted line for *solar radiation* at the point that corresponds to 500 watts/m² on the y-axis.

16. The correct answer is F. Choices G, H, and J are incorrect because *if the trend in the CH$_4$ concentration had continued to match the trend in the solar radiation intensity*, then the CH$_4$ concentration would be close to 450 ppb at present day rather than the 735 ppb that appears in Figure 2. The correct answer is F because *if the trend in the CH$_4$ concentration had continued to match the trend in the solar radiation intensity*, then the solid line in Figure 2 would be near the dotted line at all points on the graph. Since the dotted line is near a concentration of 450 ppb at the point corresponding to 0 years ago (the present), the best choice is *less than 550 ppb*.

17. The correct answer is B. Choice A is incorrect because the graph shows a decrease in CH$_4$ concentration when the temperature increases, which is the opposite of what is described in the question. Choices C and D are incorrect because they are proportional to the graph of *solar radiation* in Figure 2, not to the graph of CH$_4$ concentration. The correct answer is B because when CH$_4$ concentration increases, so does temperature. When CH$_4$ concentration decreases, temperature decreases as well. This means that the temperature graph should look similar to the graph of the solid line in Figure 2. In Figure 2, the solid line decreases then increases. The graph in choice B is the best match.

18. The correct answer is H. Choice F is incorrect because 400 watts/m² does not even appear in the range of solar radiation intensities in Figure 1. Choice G is incorrect because 440 watts/m² represents the extreme low troughs of the dotted line in Figure 1. Almost all of the dotted line occurs above this height. Choice J is incorrect because 520 watts/m² represents the upper crests of the dotted line in Figure 1. Almost all of the dotted line occurs below this threshold. The correct answer is H because the dotted line in Figure 1, which represents *solar radiation*, fluctuates relatively evenly above and below 480 watts/m², making this the best estimate for an average.

19. The correct answer is B. Choice A is incorrect because the distances between the maximum crests are greater than 15,000 years at all times in Figure 1. 15,000 would be a better estimate for the distance between each maximum and minimum, but the question did not ask for this. Choices C and D are incorrect because the distances between the maximum crests of the dotted line in Figure 1 are less than 35,000 years at all times. The correct answer is B because in Figure 1, one maximum in solar radiation intensity is found at 150 thousand years ago. The next point where the dotted line crests at a maximum is at 125 thousand years ago. This is a difference of 25,000 years. The distance between crests remains relatively constant throughout the graphs, between 20,000 and 30,000 years per maximum. The best fit for this data is *between 15,000 years and 35,000 years*.

20. The correct answer is J. Choices F and H are incorrect because the passage states that *greenhouse gases such as methane (CH$_4$) warm Earth's climate*. Choice G is incorrect because giving off *ultraviolet radiation to space* would cause the climate to cool, not warm. The correct answer is J because greenhouse gases absorb heat, causing the climate to warm.

Science Mini-Test #2

4 ○ ○ ○ ○ ○ ○ ○ ○ ○ **4**

Passage IV

In 2 experiments, a student pulled each of 3 blocks in a straight line across a flat, horizontal surface.

In Experiment 1, the student measured the *pulling force* (the force required to move each block at a constant speed) and plotted the pulling force, in newtons (N), versus block mass, in kilograms (kg). The results are shown in Figure 1.

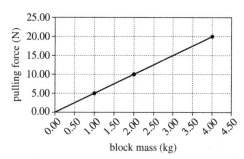

Figure 1

In Experiment 2, the student measured the speed versus time of a 2.00 kg block, a 2.50 kg block, and a 3.00 kg block as each block was pulled across the surface with a constant 30 N force. The results are shown in Figure 2.

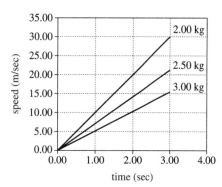

Figure 2

21. If a block was pulled toward the east, the frictional force exerted on the block by the surface was directed toward the:

A. north.
B. south.
C. east.
D. west.

22. Based on Figure 2, what is the order of the 3 blocks, from the block that required the shortest time to reach 15 m/sec to the block that required the longest time to reach 15 m/sec ?

F. 2.00 kg block, 2.50 kg block, 3.00 kg block
G. 2.00 kg block, 3.00 kg block, 2.50 kg block
H. 3.00 kg block, 2.00 kg block, 2.50 kg block
J. 3.00 kg block, 2.50 kg block, 2.00 kg block

23. Based on Figure 2, what was the approximate value of the acceleration of the 3.00 kg block?

A. 0.0 m/sec^2
B. 5.0 m/sec^2
C. 15.0 m/sec^2
D. 20.0 m/sec^2

24. Based on Figure 1, the results of Experiment 1 are best modeled by which of the following equations?

F. Block speed (m/sec) = 0.2 × time (sec)
G. Block speed (m/sec) = 5.0 × time (sec)
H. Pulling force (N) = 0.2 × block mass (kg)
J. Pulling force (N) = 5.0 × block mass (kg)

GO ON TO THE NEXT PAGE.

4 ○ ○ ○ ○ ○ ○ ○ ○ ○ **4**

25. At each of the times plotted in Figure 2 (except 0.00 sec), as block mass increased, block speed:

   A. increased only.
   B. decreased only.
   C. varied, but with no general trend.
   D. remained the same.

26. Based on Figure 1, an applied force of 30.00 N would most likely have been required to maintain the constant speed of a block having a mass of:

   F. 4.00 kg.
   G. 5.00 kg.
   H. 6.00 kg.
   J. 7.00 kg.

END OF SCIENCE MINI-TEST #2

» ANSWER EXPLANATIONS FOR SCIENCE MINI-TEST #2

21. **The correct answer is D.** Choices A and B are incorrect because the frictional force would be along the same line of motion as the object being pulled. Objects being pulled do not usually move perpendicular to the force pulling them. Choice C is incorrect because if the frictional force were in the same direction as the pulling force, friction would be *helping* the pulling, which is illogical because friction causes objects to *resist* motion. The correct answer is D because the frictional force opposes the effort to pull the block, so it would be in the opposite direction of the pulling. The opposite of east is west.

22. **The correct answer is F.** Choices G and H are incorrect because they do not accurately reflect what the graph shows about the order in which the blocks reached 15 m/sec. Choice J is incorrect because it gives the order of blocks from longest time to shortest time, the opposite of what is asked. The correct answer is F because according to Figure 2, the 2.00 kg block reached 15 m/sec in 1.5 seconds. It took the 2.50 kg block 2.1 seconds to reach 15 m/sec, and it took the 3.00 kg block just over 3 seconds to reach the same speed.

23. **The correct answer is B.** Choice A is incorrect because if the block had an acceleration of 0 m/sec^2, its speed would not increase in Figure 2. Choices C and D are incorrect because the final speed of the 3.00 kg block at 3.00 seconds was 15 m/sec, so it does not make sense to say that the block's speed increased by 15 or 20 m/sec each second. That would result in a speed of 45 or 60 m/sec after three seconds. The correct answer is B because in Figure 2, for every second on the *x*-axis, the height of the line for the 3.00 kg block increases by about 5 m/sec. This indicates an acceleration of 5 m/sec/sec, or 5 m/sec^2. Acceleration is the change in speed.

24. **The correct answer is J.** Choices F and G are incorrect because Figure 1 does not include data about block speed or time. Choice H is incorrect because, according to this formula, a block mass of 4.00 kg would require a pulling force of 0.80 N, but Figure 1 shows that it requires a pulling force of 20.00 N. The correct answer is J because this formula states that for every kg, the pulling force required increases by 5.00 N. In Figure 1, 1.00 kg corresponds to a force of 5.00 N, while 2.00 kg corresponds to a force of 10.00 N, and 4.00 kg corresponds to a force of 20.00 N. The data in Figure 1 exactly matches the formula.

25. **The correct answer is B.** Choice A is incorrect because higher masses are associated with lower speeds. Choice C is incorrect because there is a definite trend: the higher the mass, the slower the block. Choice D is incorrect because the lines for the block masses are different. If block speed remained the same, all of the lines would be on top of one another and appear as one line. The correct answer is B because, for example, at 2.00 seconds, the 2.00 kg block has a speed of 20.00 m/sec, while the 2.50 kg block has a lower speed of about 14.00 m/sec, and the heaviest 3.00 kg block has a speed of 10.00 m/sec. This relationship continues at every time frame on Figure 2. As the mass increased, the speed only decreased.

26. **The correct answer is H.** Choices F, G, and J are incorrect because these masses would correspond to pulling forces of 20.00 N, 25.00 N, and 35.00 N, respectively. The correct answer is H because in Figure 1, every kg of mass requires an additional 5.00 N of pulling force. In this figure, it can be seen that 4.00 kg corresponds to 20.00 N of pulling force. If 10.00 N is added, the weight would need to increase by 2.00 kg. Therefore, 6.00 kg is the best choice.

This page intentionally left blank.

Acknowledgements

Chief Product Officer:
Oliver Pope

Director of Curriculum:
Stephanie Constantino

Director of Quality Control:
Allison Eskind

Director of Design:
Jeff Garrett

Project Manager:
Whitney Wallace

Quality Control Coordinator:
Jesse Chasser

Cover Design:
Nicole St. Pierre

Interior Design:
Elaine Broussard
Jaye Pratt
Eliza Todorova

Test Writing:
Michael Laird

Content Creation:
Laura-Lee Alford
Jacqueline Bumler
Catherine Carney
Theresa Dash
Kerri Denholm
Amelia Emery
Alyssa Jordan
Eric Manuel
Lauren Miklovic
Justin Price
Daniel Romero
Theresa Schlafly
Mark Teel
Aubrey Trapp

Editing and Proofing:
Lauren Brecht
Dana D'Agostino
Ainsley Davis
Anne Delatte
Alicia Elley
Cassandra Galentine
Lisa Gehring
Lauren Giles
Ginny Gillikin
Miles Hamaker
Alison Hertz
Lindsey Hopton
Satchel Joseph
Michael Laird
June Manuel
AndreAnna McLean
Doug McLemore
Dylan Mulkern
Tyler Munson
Jillian Musso
Kristin Pawlowski
Rebecca Pickens
Diana Pietrogallo
Danny Ryan
Kirsten Salles
Kelly Saunier
David Schultz
Corrine Streff
Aubrey Trapp
Dawn Weldon

Boot Camp Evaluation Form

Please rate your agreement with the statements below. (1 = "Strongly Disagree" to 5 = "Strongly Agree")

My instructor was knowledgeable in the lesson content.	①	②	③	④	⑤
My instructor created an engaging learning environment.	①	②	③	④	⑤
I will be able to use what I learned when I take the test.	①	②	③	④	⑤
My confidence on the test has increased as a result of the session(s).	①	②	③	④	⑤

I would recommend MasteryPrep to someone who needs to improve their test score. Yes _____   No _____